THE NATURE OF HYSTERIA

THE NATURE
OF HYSTERIA

Niel Micklem

London and New York

First published 1996
by Routledge
11 New Fetter Lane, London EC4P 4EE

Simultaneously published in the USA and Canada
by Routledge
29 West 35th Street, New York, NY 10001

Typeset in Plantin Light by
Ponting–Green Publishing Services, Chesham, Bucks
Printed and bound in Great Britain by
T.J. Press (Padstow) Ltd, Padstow, Cornwall

British Library Cataloguing in Publication Data
A catalogue record for this book is available from
the British Library

Library of Congress Cataloguing in Publication Data
A catalogue record for this book has been requested

ISBN 0–415–12186–8

CONTENTS

To my wife, Erika

ACKNOWLEDGEMENTS

This book owes its existence, as I owe my thanks, to Molly Tuby who asked me a quarter of a century ago to talk on hysteria to the Guild of Pastoral Psychology. Since then I owe thanks to my friend, colleague and erstwhile partner, Adolf Guggenbühl-Craig for his contributions to the hysteria we managed to contain and discuss during those lunch and coffee breaks so essential to a psychiatric practice. My thanks also to Cara Denman for persuading me to publish and to my sister, Ruth Micklem, for being the only person who can read my handwriting, and so for her help with corrections in producing the manuscript of this work.

1

INTRODUCTION

Judging by any standards of pathology, hysteria must be the most extraordinary disease ever encountered by medicine. Countless generations have found in it a source of inspiration for investigation, research and discussion for the furtherance of medical science. The story of their results does not tell altogether of success or even satisfaction. On the contrary, hysteria has proved to be a source not only of inspiration, but of frustration, baffling uncertainty and downright exasperation. Furthermore, it has maintained a state of dissatisfaction and discord more persistently and for a greater length of time than any other feature of medical pathology. It cannot be surprising therefore, that amongst the foremost characteristics of hysteria is a readiness to cause suspicion in the minds of those who meet it. On many occasions throughout its history the question has arisen whether in fact hysteria should be recognised as a unit of illness. In the second half of the twentieth century the doubts and uncertainties reached a peak that motivated some medical authorities to heed the extent of their misgivings and take official action. Thereafter, in many classifications the name 'hysteria' ceased to appear as that of an illness in its own right.

The lively interest for medicine that hysteria has aroused since it was first recorded in ancient Egypt more than 3,000 years ago has yielded a substantial amount of writing. The most accomplished research worker would be hard pressed to account for all the literature, but more than enough is available to prompt the question whether there can be any grounds for yet another contribution to the field. Can there be any worthwhile aspects of hysteria left for comment? Some justification of their undertaking is due from anyone who presumes to increase this vast library if that contribution is to escape the censure of 'coals to Newcastle'.

That justification is surprisingly easy to find. A discerning and critical assessment of the present situation with regard to hysteria shows that there are at least two areas of the pathology where something more remains to be said. One of these is the need for comment on the unexpected degree of importance which hysteria has maintained in the face of repeated efforts to deny its existence. This must be judged a distinctive feature of hysteria, considering the extent of doubts about its authenticity expressed in recent centuries. Medical authority has now gone far towards establishing that hysteria is not a unit of illness, yet it continues to excite comment as such; it is referred to as frequently as ever both inside and outside the profession. The other area requiring comment concerns the old question that is now pressing more urgently for an answer: since hysteria continues to exist in spite of medical authority, what is it that exists?

The following essays take up these questions in a way that contributes towards making good yet another deficiency in the available literature, by paying particular attention to the nature of hysteria. That is not to say that no one has touched on the nature of the complaint. They have; but the deductions have for the most part been limited or obscured by the approach adopted. The majority of the investigations have been, directly or indirectly, the work of the medical profession and approached accordingly in an empirical manner appropriate to medical study. Even the more recent contributions from psychologists show evidence of the same influence, having been approached largely through the perspective of a psychology shaped by medicine. They have provided a comprehensive documentation of clinical details about hysteria throughout all the phases of its long existence, together with many theories and explanations of what it is. Few particulars have been overlooked and there is little room for criticism of this conscientious work. Nevertheless, there is a significant limitation in this research and that is a factor which must be taken into consideration here, for it has immediate bearing on the necessity for these essays. It is well known, though not always very consciously, that medicine wields a formidable power. Fear of illness and the corresponding degree of dependency on physicians ensure that this power remains undisputed and largely unquestioned. As a result, much is taken for granted and some of medicine's limitations are overlooked and neglected to the detriment of both patient and physician. The medical approach to pathology is one such undisputed factor and one which has a special relevance for this discussion on hysteria in as much as its first and foremost concern is with the manifestations of hysteria in patients and – though it might well be hotly denied – only indirectly concerned with hysteria itself. That oversight has brought familiarity with the appearances and the effects of eccentric presentations, but relatively little about the essence of hysteria itself. It is as if some elusive quality within that disease has a way of obscuring the view. The many unsuccessful attempts of medicine to tie it down have meant that hysteria is denied and rejected for not being what it ought to be instead of being recognised for what it is.

The orthodox approach to the investigation of disease as recognised by the medical profession is not the only way of viewing the pathologies of human existence; but, before introducing an alternative, it is well to have in mind a picture of those characteristics which are in general understood as typical of hysteria. A precise description is a difficult undertaking, for hysteria is protean: a multifaced disease presenting such a wide variety of appearances that it has earned the reputation in some circles of being an absurd ailment with a fair proportion of incomprehensible symptoms. Nevertheless, it has also established to some extent an image consistent enough to have gained recognition as hysteria. This image must fall short on accuracy because it is scientifically structured in a way that has not taken into consideration the long history of the disease. In the minds of many, hysteria starts rather vaguely in the nineteenth century when it was recognised as a prominent form of neurotic illness and the earlier history, spanning a period of millennia, counts for little.

From these comparatively recent beginnings, closely associated with the French neurologist, Jean-Martin Charcot (1835–93), hysteria has remained firmly a manifestation of neurotic illness to the extent that the two words, 'hysteria' and 'neurosis', have become vaguely interchangeable.

The widespread, popular impression of hysteria is itself a slightly 'hysterical' exaggeration of accounts found in the textbooks of medicine. Broadly speaking, hysteria has come to mean two different states: the demonstration of uncontrollable outbursts on the one hand and, on the other, an illness that in some way is not quite genuine. With regard to that illness, symptoms may be mental or physical or both together. The physical symptoms command the singular characteristic of being able to imitate those of almost any illness, but, in keeping with the nature of neurosis, the hysteria is distinguished from the others by the absence of organic cause. For example, hysteria may appear as blindness, deafness, skin anaes-thesia, paralysis, spasm, tremor and countless other presentations; but so, too, may many infections, poisonings, allergies, growths and such like aetiologies. Hysteria needs differentiation from those 'genuine' illnesses with their physical symptoms resulting from organic causes.

It is surprising how often the word 'genuine' arises in connection with hysteria; the presence of the disease raises suspicion, followed quickly by a moral censure that hysteria is a fraudulent complaint. Supporting the suspicion of fraudulence there is the so-called hysteric personality which may accompany the physical symptoms or exist independently. A cardinal feature is the high degree of emotionality encountered and the need to exaggerate. Such people desire to be more than they really are and combine their fanciful approach to life with considerable skill in self-deception. Suggest-ibility is a notable characteristic that carries with it a remarkable capacity for identification with, and imitation of, others. It is widely assumed that all hysteria is a demonstration to achieve some gains for the subject.

Much of this picture, though by no means all, is the result of Freud's studies in hysteria from the end of the nineteenth century.

Freud not only regarded hysteria as a neurosis, but made it the central feature in his theory of neurosis as well as the cornerstone on which to found psychoanalysis. Yet, in spite of Freud's comprehensive classification of the neuroses, hysteria has remained an uncertain, controversial quantity. To the extent that a distinct syndrome of hysteria is recognised, it can be summed up in short as a neurotic illness with pronounced features of suggestibility; with an emotional instability and readiness to fall into psychic dissociation, so that conflict is often converted unconsciously into physical symptoms; with a tendency towards flight into illness if things go wrong; with an exaggeration of expression and over-relatedness towards spectators, much of which stems from a desire to be 'at the centre of the stage', cost what it may.

Whether in fact this rough account of hysteria is the outcome of medical researches from past centuries, or only those of recent decades, it is certainly that of a scientific, medical approach to pathology. In the following essays a different approach is adopted. The essays, though written with the knowledge of a physician, are in the first place psychological rather than medical–psychological works. The focus of attention is not on what the signs and symptoms have to say about hysteria, but on the image of hysteria and what this has to say about the signs and symptoms. It is not the customary approach to an illness; not a search for causes, cures and explanations so much as for meaning within the essential conditions of the state. It is in other words an archetypal approach to a medical subject: a study in the reading of an image. Let it be clearly understood at the outset that this does not replace, or attempt to render obsolete, the already existing works of many centuries. On the contrary, it complements the more scientific counterpart and brings with it in this instance some rewarding insights and added significance to the signs and symptoms of this enigmatic disease.

This work with the image of hysteria may be likened – approximately, but appropriately – to that in analytic psychotherapy of listening to a dream or equivalent expression of the imagination. The dream image, like that of hysteria, speaks to and with the imagination in a manner that allows for dialogue. That is to say, to avoid prejudgement, and before contemplating any amplification of the material, it is of the utmost importance to hear all the image has to say about itself. Such an undertaking, simple though it may sound, is far from easy. The trap for the unwary of making the interpretation before listening to the interpretation is a very real and ever present hazard. In the present study there is a further difficulty, that a direct confrontation with the image of hysteria means an encounter with a singular characteristic little appreciated by observers: the tendency of hysteria to disappear from sight suddenly and without warning.

The essentially psychological approach of reading an image is not everywhere granted the degree of respect to which it is entitled. Far from it. Studying psychopathology by way of the image in this way means approaching it as psychological necessity, the very idea of which is alone enough to deter many workers. It may awaken some interest, but is rarely taken seriously, expecially when set beside the expectations held out by the approach of medical science that presumes to eliminate pathologies. To a surprising degree it is taken for granted that the medical approach through scientific, empirical observation is the only way toward a serious or important contribution to the clinical literature. A psychological approach, unless it follows the accustomed medical pattern, is in danger of rejection, of dismissal as an indulgence in fanciful reflections or vague practices of meditation; in any case, of having no serious bearing on clinical matters, as if the word clinical excluded psychology. Yet this work in psychology is not only serious in itself, but is a serious and necessary contribution towards complementing the limitations of clinical observation on illness. How and where it differs from conventional medical writing is apparent and speaks for itself. It stands in no need of justification, for the outcome of the study is very rewarding in the wealth of material it contributes to the existing medical appreciation of hysteria.

2

CHANGING CULTURE

If there were ever doubts that there is artistry in the science of medicine, the responsibilities of diagnosis alone would dispel them. Under one hospital roof may be found a wide variety of ailments in an assortment of patients who, though referred to different departments, are suffering from the same disease: hysteria. In the medical out-patient department is a schoolgirl with headaches and described as childish, a 'dreamer', versatile, impressionable and uncooperative. She does not appear to be very ill and there is little enough to go on, but in this context the characteristics of personality coupled with the headaches is called hysteria. Also in the department of medicine a 30-year-old man recently went blind and soon afterwards developed a weakness of the right hand. It would not be far off the mark for a physician to think in terms of an early multiple sclerosis, but the case history says that this is a man suffering from hysteria. In the department of neurology a man recovered from an epileptic fit is cause for further diagnostic surprise. The report says this fit was no epilepsy; he, like the man with blindness, is suffering from hysteria. But what of the woman in the department of obstetrics with the large belly of a nine-months pregnancy? There is no sign of a foetus in the womb. Could this, too, be hysteria? It sounds highly suggestive. But no; this rather unexpected diagnosis is merely pseudocyesis.

The details of the cases mentioned here are wholly inadequate as medical reports, yet there is sufficient to realise that something surprising, if not downright disconcerting, has appeared in the field of medical practice. The diagnoses are not quite convincing; even in the case of the 'pregnant' woman where hysteria was not mentioned, there is a suspicion that she, unlike the other patients, probably was suffering from the disease known as hysteria. The picture does not inspire confidence and there is more than a hint of deception. What exactly is this ubiquitous and many-featured disease called hysteria? Judging by the frequent use of the word, most people seem to know, yet no one can define or diagnose it convincingly.

These four abbreviated examples from hospital practice alone give sufficient evidence that hysteria is no ordinary ailment. The variation and the apparent unrelatedness of signs and symptoms mark it as an exception in the classifications of disease. In his book *Diseases of the Nervous System* Sir Francis Walshe (1895–1973) commented on this theme that, 'there is . . . no symptom complex of somatic illness that may not have its hysterical "double"' (1963, p. 361). He was merely repeating what others before him had formulated in different words as, for example, when Thomas Sydenham (1624–89), the distinguished physician of the seventeenth century, observed that, 'the shapes of Proteus and the colours of the chameleon are not more numerous and inconsistent than the variations of hysteria disease' (Whyatt 1767, p. 95). W. Johnson, a physician of the nineteenth century, went so far as to call hysteria 'the mocking bird of nosology' (Johnson 1849, p. 5). These authors were writing of a veritable trickster in the textbooks of pathology.

Medical historians record a long and fascinating tale. Although the immediate interest here is in the nature rather than the presentation of hysteria, the history calls for a brief look, the better to appreciate that subject whose nature is under review. For purposes of convenience it may be divided into four periods: classical antiquity, mediaeval witchcraft, modern neurology and contemporary psychology. All are of equal importance and each distinguishes well-defined changes in the presentation of appearances of hysteria.

The history of this disease tells of many different signs and symptoms as well as a variety of different causes. It is a story involving deception and intrigue, immorality, heresy, mistrust, intolerance and much irritation, sometimes reading more like a novel than an account of an illness. Though the changing features may seem unrelated, there is in fact a thread, often ill-defined and difficult to recognise, running throughout the long history. It brings a degree of consistency to the assortment of features, linking the changes as if they were extravagant variations on an underlying theme.

The earliest references to hysteria appeared in the second millennium BC. They described a gynaecological disorder, a disease of women with many different and diffuse symptoms and signs. In otherwise healthy women – usually a maiden, spinster or widow – these included shallow breathing with a sensation of suffocation; palpitations; a weak pulse; pallor and a cold, clammy skin; belching and sometimes vomiting; contortions of the body with convulsive fits or loss of consciousness in a flaccid body; headaches and loss of sight, speech or memory. Though the signs and symptoms were noticeably diffuse, their cause was localised in the pelvis in a womb separated from its moorings. Independent of the genital tract, the womb wandered the body cavity causing widespread symptoms through pressure and suffocation in various organs; in particular, when lodged in the upper thorax as the *globus hystericus*, it was responsible for impeding the flow of air and for the sensation of suffocation. Hence the name, 'hysteric suffocation'.

The treatments recommended for this ailment emphasised its sexual nature. They consisted largely of good counsel directed towards finding a man, lover or husband, with the idea ultimately of impregnation for the barren womb. Together with this advice, various procedures were recommended to seduce and force the womb back to its natural setting. A mixture of sweet-smelling ingredients was burned with intent to fumigate the vulva and seduce the womb, while foul smells were inhaled from above to drive it downwards into the pelvis.

The pattern of hysteria prevailed with but slight variations for several centuries. In time a more accurate understanding of human anatomy threw doubt on the wandering of the womb; but this did little more than raise other theories of how the womb caused hysteria. The womb was a fixture in the pelvis, but liable to change in size and shape as it filled with spirit in some way as a result of retained female secretions. Transmission of the retained material by way of blood or nerves was understood to be the origin of the suffocation. This slight change in the aetiology was yet sufficient for some writers to suggest that hysteria might not be limited only to women. At the time the idea failed to gain a wide acceptance and was not taken seriously until a much later period of history.

Serious illness in antiquity was to a great extent attributed directly to divine influence; its treatment was largely miraculous. A more scientific approach grew in the fifth century BC during the Hippocratic era of medicine, when natural causes for disease began to gain recognition. This more sophisticated view of sickness thrived until mediaeval history recorded a tendency to revert to the previous attitude. Belief in divine causes returned to some extent, but this time with the emphasis on evil spirits, demons and sorcerers. Hysteria was, alone amongst diseases, singled out as belonging specifically to the domain of witches. As this coincided with the period in history when witches were burned at the stake as heretics, it meant that medicine was responsible for the extension of an already widespread persecution of women. The historic events have become so familiar that it is easy, though quite incorrect, to assume that hysteria came under the immediate jurisdiction of the Inquisition. In fact the handling of hysteria was a matter for the courts temporal rather than spiritual; but there is little doubt, none the less, that the influence of the inquisitorial treatment of witches spread beyond the Church. To some extent hysteria had ceased to be an ordinary disease in need of medical treatment and had begun to look like a crime, even a sin, in need of punishment.

During this time of inexcusable prejudice, the familiar signs and symptoms of hysteria continued largely unaltered, though a strong emphasis falling on hysteric anaesthesia of the skin marked a slight modulation. Areas of the body surface found to be lacking in sensation were used as confirmation of hysteria and condemnation of the witch. The heightened state of emotionality, never far away when hysteria is present, stood out as a collective phenomenon of note during this phase of its history. It spread like an infection as the wave of emotion blinded patients, physicians, witches and the legal authorities alike. That any circumstances could allow the appalling atrocities to take place is strongly suggestive of a mass hysteria dominating the scene.

The next major change to take place in hysteria came with the return of scientific authority in medical thought as the Renaissance approached. Some forms of mental ill health were regarded as states of possession by spirits, but the causes of disease in general had moved far from the idea of a direct, divine influence. Hysteria returned wholly into the keeping of medicine, to be treated as best befitted an organically caused disease. One noticeable advancement of immediate relevance was the recognition of neurology and its rise to a new importance. Hysteria remained to some extent a disease of the womb, but the centre of its pathology now found a home in the nervous system; it became primarily a neurological, rather than a gynaecological, complaint. More precisely, hysteria became a disorder of the head. The cause of the pathology was believed to lie in the brain, but it maintained in some way a sympathetic interaction with the womb.

After many centuries as a disorder of the womb, this shift of location from the pelvis to the head was a momentous step. A long overdue change in the medical image was taking place. There is no mistaking the symbolic significance of the anatomical findings: the cause of hysteria moved from the psychologically instinctive level of the pelvis to the intellectual and spiritual heights of the head, meaning that it was more readily available for conscious understanding. The new seat of cause could be claimed, at least theoretically, by either sex. Eventually the scientific (but not the imaginative) ties with the womb weakened to such an extent that a way opened up for physicians to accept the idea proposed many centuries earlier by Galen of Pergamon (AD 129–99) and others that hysteria was not a disease limited exclusively to women. But it proved to be only an opening. That the problem was never one for pure, rational science is confirmed by the astonishing weight of prejudice yet to be overcome before sex equality in hysteria could be truly accepted.

As an intermediary step on the way to a more acceptable sex

distribution, Thomas Sydenham discovered that hypochondriasis was the form hysteria took in men. In retrospect this rather unconvincing addition of a new name raises a suspicion that vanity might have prompted its appearance to spare man from too close and too quick an identity with an established woman's complaint. But such vanity cannot have been the only motive behind the idea, for hypochondriasis established itself with a comparable authority and in time demonstrated a closer affinity with hysteria than that noted originally by Sydenham. The name referred to a suffocation of the spleen and other abdominal organs of the area around the midriff known as the hypochondria. A connection with hysteria lasted until recent times, though the image of hypochondriasis changed in the meantime to that of a melancholy and morbid preoccupation with health in general. It presented with a high degree of suggestibility and a tendency to self-hypnosis, characteristics it shared in common with certain unchanging aspects of hysteria.

The growth of neurology brought with it an increasing awareness of affect and its significance for illness. The close correlation of emotion with the nervous system – later localised more precisely in the autonomic nervous system – was not limited to physical disorders, but proved to be a phenomenon directing attention towards a broader understanding of mental health. With regard to hysteria, the acute physical suffering of the patients was regarded in many instances as a form of insanity. Demonic possession was still the cause of that indefinite state, insanity, but it is not difficult to see in these developments how emotion and the nervous system were pointing the way to a more scientific appreciation of insanity as psychosis, a disturbance of the mind that was later understood in terms of the psyche.

The role of the nervous system in the transmission of emotion, mediating between psychic and physical realms, opened the door to the next big transformation for hysteria, carrying it into the present era.

The evidence of history shows that hysteria was never true to any one particular department of medicine for long. It now moved from neurology into the newly discovered field of neurosis. In this latest venture, hysteria did not abandon altogether the physical side of medicine, but, with neurosis as a stepping stone, it began to establish a place in psychology. Hysteria fitted easily and comfortably into the category of functional illness; with an unobtrusive collusion, it soon became virtually synonymous with neurosis. There has never been a more serious medical interest shown in this unusual disease than in its close association with neurosis in the nineteenth century. In the minds of many, that is where hysteria began and where it remained. Every student of psychology knows that Sigmund Freud (1856–1939) built psychoanalysis on hysteria and through it defined the most comprehensive theory of neurosis ever to appear. After several thousand years, hysteria had changed its pattern of sexuality from a dissociation of womb activity to a dissociation of repressed infantile sexuality. In this way hysteria became a fundamental feature of the psychoneuroses.

C. G. Jung (1875–1961) also regarded hysteria as a neurosis, but with his own broader view of this term. In his early work as a psychiatrist, he commented that there is no clear line of demarcation between hysteria, neurosis and some little understood somnambulist states (1902, p. 3). Jung brought to hysteria far greater significance than it received from Freud by emphasising that it was not simply a negative phenomenon of destructive tendencies. He considered that, in keeping with neurosis in general, hysteria held constructive possibilities, even that it possessed qualities which under other circumstances could point to genius. Hysteria was more than a disease to be cured, being a necessary ingredient of the personality and a state that, for him, was readily understandable in terms of the psychological complex. For Jung this was one amongst many features of the personality, having a significant archetypal background and a potential of affect capable of causing distress or disease and the need for psychotherapy.

Hysteria continues to exist in the field of psychology, but, as a unit of disease in its own right, it has vanished from medicine. Nevertheless, as mentioned in the introduction, it has established a lasting image based, prior to its disappearance, on descriptions in most textbooks of medicine. Hysteria was described as a disease of the

13

mind and the body in which an hysteric personality might exist on its own or be accompanied by a variety of physical symptoms. These outward manifestations of hysteria could mimic any organic illness without any signs of a corresponding organic pathology or of anxiety. The hysteric personality was a complex structure. It was regarded as egocentric, immature and demanding. Behaviour tended to be theatrical with a display designed to impress as well as gain attention and sympathy. There was little evidence of an ability to sustain attention, but a compensatory ability to day-dream. The subjects of these characteristics were noted to be sexually frigid though, in sharp contrast to the earlier history, sexuality was not considered to be of aetiological significance. In general, these temperamental people were regarded as having carried an infantile need for exclusive love and attention into their adult life.

Clearly there is room for doubt whether this medical assessment describes a true unit of disease or an ill-defined assortment of features belonging to several other syndromes. The qualities of the personality outlined are not convincing; they could as well be those of any recognised neurotic development. With a stretch of the imagination, the physical symptoms attributed to hysteria might have been ex-plained as modifications of Freud's conversion hysteria, but it would have been without sufficient credibility for medical science. In fact it is not surprising that official classifications of disease decided to omit the term hysteria and substitute conversion symptom for those physical ailments previously known as conversion hysteria.

Whatever hysteria may be, it still stands somewhere between medicine and psychology. Since the decision not to recognise it as a disease in its own right, the name continues vaguely in medicine in the adjectival form, 'hysteric', as it did in those far away times of hysteric suffocation. In some ways hysteria may have forfeited respect, but not vitality. One way or another it survives, though no longer carrying serious diagnostic implications. More often it is used irresponsibly and inaccurately in situations of diagnostic uncertainty; sometimes even as a term of abuse. In either case hysteria is not yet dead.

In conventional terms of illness this brief historic outline tells an extraordinary tale. No disease can have changed its features so much through the centuries and yet maintained some consistent and recognisable identity; few can have presented such difficulties for medicine and defied attempts at definition for so long. Is this really a disease or something more than is normally understood by that term? The changes it has undergone did not, as might be assumed, take place at random or simply to satisfy the whims of scientific minds. They leave an impression of inevitability and follow patterns that are almost predictable from certain threads running throughout its history. It is by no means clear whether medical science has been responsible for changing hysteria or whether hysteria has changed the face of medicine, if not indeed of whole cultural scenes in which it has existed.

It has long been known that the anatomical claim of a wandering womb as the cause of hysteria is scientifically far from accurate; yet the persistence with which this idea was held and taught for centuries is in itself a remarkable phenomenon not to be dismissed lightly. There are grounds for thinking it must have carried, and in some way still does carry, a greater significance than physicians are willing to admit. Let this singular idea recorded long ago, that the wandering womb is the cause of hysteria, be readmitted once again for reflection. The idea, the psychic fact born of an image is not in itself true or false. Latter-day science has assessed it as inaccurate and follows its own truth, but that does not mean its old truth ceases to exist. It remains as a psychological reality behind the changing scientific assessment. This strange phenomenon persists in calling for attention and for a better understanding of the nature of hysteria, as if that ancient and venerable disease had not yet gained satisfaction.

3

THE MYTH OF HYSTERIA

A myth of ancient Greece tells how the womb as mother in a state of frustration and anger wanders the body of woman causing disease with suffocation. An even older myth with the same Mediterranean origins tells how the mother in a state of grief and anger wanders the earth and sea searching for the maiden taken from her. The account of the earth wanderer, the myth of Eleusis, is told by the poet Homer, though Heroditus suggests that it appeared earlier in Egypt. That of the body wanderer, the myth of hysteria and the wandering womb, is told by the physician Hippocrates, though recorded earlier in Egyptian papyri.

These tales form a part of the vast mythology of the mother and are the main subject matter of this work on hysteria. One is a divine myth of gods and goddesses; the other is a human myth of the mother in relation to other aspects of woman. A cursory glance is enough to see that the two belong together in a special way; that the similarities of origin, content and pattern establish a close kinship. The question is, what special relevance does this kinship carry for hysteria? Sharing so many features in common, these two myths are drawn together. They react on each other like two people in a dialogue that can enlighten their respective areas of darkness. In other words, a study in contrast of the two myths is a way of illuminating some dark areas of the psychopathologies they reflect. It is, of course, especially relevant to this work that somewhere between the two lies a pattern which reveals itself as hysteria.

The history of hysteria's changing face in changing cultures makes a fascinating tale of a disease whose features lend themselves with readiness to publicity and yet remain to a large extent a mystery. It reads like a story, almost like the unfolding plot of a drama where the curtain has not yet fallen on the last act. Not just the history, but the myth of hysteria also, reads like a story, but with a difference. History is the story of recorded events, though they are seen through the myths of memory. Myth, on the other hand, is the story written in itself. It, too, is fascinating and leaves a feeling of mystery in that the story is never quite finished. The myth and the history complement each other, though it might not be immediately obvious why the myth warrants attention when the facts of history are already established.

Myth and history also complement each other in diseases where, in a markedly scientific age, myth has forfeited respect and meaning. The customary use of the word 'myth' implies that a situation is not quite real, a matter of lesser importance and not to be taken seriously. Indeed, to speak of illness in the same breath as myth is to invite ridicule. The remark, 'that's just a myth', is a sad reflection on the way imagination is underrated. Yet myth is the psyche's mode of expression, familiar to the extent of being taken for granted in dreams and much undervalued in the waking state of consciousness. The imagery of myth is the psyche's language of communication and the source of all experience, of which those in sickness are no exception. For disease is not simply a fault appearing in the body but is, at the same time, the myth of the individual soul expressed and experienced in the body.

To say that every disease is a myth as well as a display of signs and symptoms has no derogatory implications; it is not to say that the ailment is not real or merely is a figment of hypochondriacal fantasy. It restates that there is a psychic image within the manifestation of illness giving form and spontaneity of expression. The onset, the signs and the symptoms may be utterly meaningless to the one whose life has been disrupted; but there is an archetypal structure behind those seemingly random disturbances so that they play their parts none the less in shaping the destiny of the individual.

But myth, as well as shaping the individual, also makes the mythology of individual diseases. This aspect of pathology is rarely taken into consideration, though it is striking in some instances. The well-known malady of low back pain is a ready example. It had certainly been a scourge of humankind for many centuries before it established an identity as 'railway back' in the nineteenth century after the arrival of steam trains. It also became lumbago, fibrositis of the spine, synovitis of spinal joints, slipped discs and several other images of the events determining the recurrent pain. Each is based on some reliable authority of responsible medical investigation and together they account for a mythology of low back pain. A similar pattern exists in the changing emphasis on various biochemical findings with regard to food stuffs in disease, especially those concerned with the heart and circulation. The potentials for cure and for good health are in no way undermined by attention to this side of illness. On the contrary, a recognition of myth enhances the authority of disease by confirming its place as a psychic reality and saving it from the discredit of being nothing more than the effects of an external agent, an inadvertent blemish on an idea of 'good health'. As well as enhancing respect for disease, it brings awareness of the psychic factor shaping the science of medicine.

In spite of a well-documented history of hysteria, the myth of this disease warrants attention because myth tells of the origins of its being rather than of its historic beginnings, descriptions, explanations, causes and cures. If the need for that approach can be grasped, it confirms the impression gained from the experience of many centuries, that many people when discussing hysteria do not, in the truest sense of the words, know what they are talking about. That may sound dismissive, but it is not an idle criticism of people's intelligence so much as an observation pertaining specifically to hysteria. The nature, and with it the values, the implications and the very significance of this disease, have not been recognised. References to this feature are markedly lacking in the literature of hysteria.

An enquiry into the myth of hysteria to discern its meaning is, first and foremost, a study in psychopathology; but, unlike most studies in that field, the foremost intent is not to discern the meaning it brings to the patient or sufferer. In this instance the centre of attention is the disease itself. The two are easily confused and the emphasis for study falls in the wrong place. An extension of this oversight leads to another area that stands in need of discrimination when studying this or any other psychopathology. Attention directed towards the myth of a disease is not the same as attention directed towards any mythological images which may be reflected in that disease. The significance of that distinction may not be immediately apparent, yet it is a matter of the utmost importance. The rich symbolism of mythologies has become a familiar feature in the practice of psychology, and familiarity breeds, if not contempt, at least carelessness. It is used frequently for the amplification of motifs that may appear in the course of psychotherapy. But the work of amplification on a motif is not the same procedure as the reading of an image whereby that image interprets itself. They are different practices, though often mistaken for each other.

By way of example, an analytic psychotherapist writes of treating an hysteric woman, 'I found myself thinking . . . in terms of the Demeter–Persephone myth' (Williams 1956, p. 179). This is the approach of amplification and is of undisputed value in certain therapeutic situations. It is at the same time diametrically opposite to that adopted here. Direction is the significant factor: not from a syndrome of disease to myth, but from a myth to its manifestation as a disease syndrome. The chosen example is of particular relevance for this study. It refers to Demeter and Persephone and the myth of Eleusis which is often a rewarding amplification for many aspects of psychopathology, including hysteria. Yet, in spite of striking resemblances, the myth of Eleusis is not that of hysteria. In view of their similarities, the differentiation of the two is essential for the understanding of hysteria.

The discovery many centuries ago that a wandering womb was the cause of hysteric disease proved later to be anatomically senseless and a literal impossibility. Yet long after physicians had established the anatomical error, the womb continued to influence the image of hysteria. How this aetiological error maintained its effectiveness through the centuries is one of the wonders of medicine. Its persistence is a hint that there may be more in this pathology than the value of a literal meaning, that there is in fact an element of myth in the wandering womb. That image holds the diverse manifestations of this singular disease as it has appeared through the centuries. It is the thread that places them naturally in their historic settings, not as disconnected events in the progress of science, but as 'reincarnations', as variations on a theme which together make the mythology of hysteria.

A new and unexpected interest arises when the womb is no longer restricted by its role in medicine. For purposes of physiological and anatomical descriptions it is the uterus, a pelvic organ which possesses epithelial and muscular tissues of extraordinary qualities in relation to pregnancy. But the womb is at the same time a central feature of woman's body, expressing qualities pertaining to the mother. In an earlier use of the language the two words, 'womb' and 'mother', shared the same meaning to a greater extent than they do today; they were to some degree interchangeable. Today their meanings are separate, but without altering the fact that the wandering of the womb is the wandering of the mother and that displacement of the mother with suffocation is hysteria, the disease known as the 'suffocation of the mother'.

The tale of the wandering womb is a myth and the purpose of this work is to observe its image closely in order to hear what it says about hysteria throughout its long clinical history. But, before turning to the myth, it is well to clarify a feature of the womb that threatens to undermine the authenticity of its message.

In the practice of gynaecology a physician meets various states of local uterine displacement as well as other disorders of the uterus which make their appearances far removed from the pelvis as, for example, when the endometrium sets up metastases in other parts of the body. It may be argued that these 'uterine wanderings' are the present-day equivalent of the earlier womb disorder. That is not the case; the pathologies in question belong to other disease entities known respectively as prolapse uteri and endometriosis. They carry only distant associations with hysteria and none at all with the myth of the womb. Any endeavour to fit them into the image of the wandering womb could only distort the image of hysteria, for the wandering of the mother does not carry the same significance as the wandering of a uterus.

A threat of further misunderstanding lies, not with the pathology of the uterus, but with the psychology of the womb. In the practice of psychotherapy the motif of the mother has grown to assume an exaggerated importance in both cause and treatment of disorders. The mother, in one form or another, seems to be everywhere. Can it be that hysteria turns out after all to be yet another example of the psychotherapist's obsessive theme, the 'negative mother', the much used and abused explanation of every psychopathology, difficulty or displeasure of human beings in recent times? If that were the cause of hysteria, it could well be hailed as her oldest and finest champion. But no; even the name 'suffocation of the mother' cannot detract from the message given by the myth. Although a feature of central importance in hysteria, there is no indication that the motif of the mother is the cause or explanation of the pathology. But the role is ambiguous. It is not clearly stated whether the mother has been ousted from her natural situation or whether she seeks of her own volition to cause unrest elsewhere. The myth tells of the mother in relation to the rest of woman's psychic constitution and how this reflects in woman's body. There can be no question of negative causes here without consideration of the rest of archetypal woman. Whatever causes may be relevant to the hysteria situation, the image of the goddesses is not the cause of the hysteria; it is the hysteria.

The myth of hysteria is told simply and concisely by Plato where he writes in the 'Timaeus', 'The womb . . . when it remains barren too long after puberty, is distressed and sorely disturbed and, straying about the body and cutting off the passages of breath, it impedes respiration' (1892, p. 514). There are no details of any events; only the symptomatic evidence of suffocation suggests that some encounter has taken place. In contrast to this austere account of the mother, Homer, in his hymn to Demeter, tells in considerable detail of the background to the wandering. This hymn, the myth of Eleusis, describes encounters with other characters who, though not mentioned directly, are essentially contained in the hysteria myth.

With the firm reminder that Homer's poetry is not a mythic account of hysteria, it is a great help to note that the features portrayed by the hymn are the most immediate and satisfactory way to gain acquaintance with those characters not emphasised in the myth of hysteria.

Homer's hymn is the tale of the great threefold goddess of Greek myth who appears as Demeter, Persephone and Hecate. It is best known for the opening passages, describing the rape of Persephone. In it the *Kore*, the goddess maiden known as Persephone, strays from the mother and, while playing with other maidens, is raped by the underworld god Hades in the form of Pluto. The mother as Demeter wanders the earth and sea in search. A third form of the same divinity, the moon goddess Hecate, has heard the cries of rape and helps to discover the place of abduction. After the rape events will never be the same again. Demeter mourns her loss, assumes a human form and, in her wrath, contrives that no crops will grow. The inevitable famine from this blight on the earth is experienced indirectly by Zeus when his starving people no longer make sacrifices to him. Demeter demands the restoration of her daughter and Zeus reacts to the crisis with a compromise; he rules that Persephone will spend one-third of each year with her underworld spouse and the remaining two-thirds with her mother. Hecate becomes her constant companion.

The mother as she appears in the myth of hysteria must be seen to be the same great threefold goddess, and this brief resumé of Homer's hymn to Demeter shows where the characteristics of that goddess may be discovered. To discover those characteristics means an exacting study of reading the image. This is never an easy exercise and carries an additional difficulty in this context: of the many qualities attributed to hysteria, none is more prominent than its potential for deception. That quality resides in the myth. The disease, hysteria, appears for diagnosis in various forms only to bewilder the physician in the next moment by seeming no longer to be there; or, at least, not in the form that a moment previously had seemed so convincing. Doubts appear in plenty. Is that a demonstration of an exaggerated suggestibility hysteria or is it that of an artistic sensibility under some unusual pressure? Is that extravagant and uncontrolled display of emotion really hysteria or is it seen through a prejudice that assumes unconsciously that all undesirable outbreaks of emotion are hysteria? Must the patient with convulsions be suffering from hysteria if the diagnosis is not epilepsy or may it be a simple vegetative disturbance with loss of consciousness? There are ample grounds for this uncertainty simply in the confusing way the myth of hysteria both is and is not the myth of Eleusis.

In itself the myth of hysteria reads as an uncomplicated and apparently simple tale; but the fullness of its meaning is far from easy to grasp. It is, for example, far from obvious that the hysteric womb in its relation to woman is a reflection of the great threefold goddess, though that knowledge is of the utmost importance for an understanding of hysteria. Previously unnoticed features of hysteria make their appearance in relief in the light of contrast between the two myths. That contrast gives form to the following essays.

4

COLD COMFORT

An outstanding feature of hysteria's myth is its setting exclusively in the framework of woman. All details of the tale are limited to the female sex with no mention whatsoever of man's presence. Small wonder that for centuries hysteria was accepted as a disease of woman only; indeed, how could it have been otherwise when man does not possess a womb? Any recognition of hysteria in the other sex must surely imply that the diagnosis is incorrect.

There are intimations early in the history of hysteria that women were not the only sufferers and that perhaps men, too, were subject to the disease; but the idea was far from convincing and scarcely heard. Not until the advancements made in science during the sixteenth century was there any official recognition of hysteria appearing in man as well as woman, and even then the old prejudice lingered. Doubtless there were some who maintained the exclusiveness of woman's claim up to the end of hysteria's recognition as a disease; but those early intimations that man, too, could bear the marks were none the less justified. In whatever form it may present, it is clear today that hysteria is not a gynaecological illness as such, but the reflection in the body of an exclusively female archetypal pattern; a mythic expression of the mother in relation to the rest of archetypal woman. This psychology must surely belong as much to man as to woman.

The myth of hysteria and the wandering womb is a medical tale formulated in the traditional language of anatomy. Like a dream, it touches the imagination and, like a dream, the idiom is metaphoric although the language makes it sound more like a literal pathology within the anatomic bounds. In other words, it is important, in order to avoid misunderstanding, to bear in mind that the image speaks of the significance rather than the explanation of the anatomy in hysteric pathology. The theme of the myth implies a disruption within the genital tract; a womb separated from its moorings in the pelvis and wandering the cavity of the body. It implies that the roots of the womb in the upper end of the vagina have been dislodged, leaving that portion of woman's anatomy to lead an autonomous and dissociated existence. If anatomically unconvincing, the picture is correspondingly rewarding as a symbolic expression. It portrays the crucial relations between the womb with its cervix and the vagina with its hymen; that is to say, between the mother and the maiden. In the language of anatomy, the wandering implies that the upper end of the vagina has been torn while the introitus – the hymen and thus the natural site for tearing – remains intact. The 'wrong' end is involved and a natural process distorted.

The motifs of mother, maiden and wandering are common to the myths of both hysteria and Eleusis. The superficial likenesses between the two are striking, though a close look at the contrast shows differences, some of which are equally striking while others, being less obtrusive, are overlooked. For example, the mother and the maiden undergo separation in each of the myths; yet there is a difference in the manner of separation which alters the whole meaning of the images. In the myth of Eleusis, these two figures are destined from all time to be together, even though separation must enter into the picture. It is in fact a paradoxical feature of this timeless image that, even in separation, the togetherness remains. For they are but two aspects of the same thing. The hysteric myth tells a different tale. The separation takes place, but without the paradox of the two remaining together. However much they may seem to be destined for togetherness, they are, in this separation, no longer aspects of the same thing, but two different and very determined ways of being. The effect in general is sterile and unrelated. The myth describes a barren situation to be compared with a pseudocyesis that has all the external appearance of a real pregnancy, but without the fruit of conception. The separations in these myths might be mistaken for each other in much the same way that hysteria in clinical practice is itself easily mistaken for other diseases.

A degree of violence accompanies the separation of mother and maiden and this, like so many other shared features, is described in more detail in the myth of Eleusis where the motif of the *rape* stands in the foreground. It introduces a male figure into the otherwise exclusively female setting.

Not only is the rape outstanding and eye-catching, but its absence in the other myth points directly to the feature that stamps hysteria like a hallmark engraved on all aspects of that disease. As this absence proves to be a matter of such singular importance, it becomes a matter of equal importance to discern as precisely as possible the features of all that is missing; in other words, the features of the rape. It proves to be an exacting task of psychological investigation which concerns Hades in the form of Pluto as well as the great threefold goddess in all her aspects.

Rape in a sexually permissive society has become a provocative subject. In hysteria it is as much concerned with sex as in any other context, but it presents in a setting where for once it is possible to grasp that sex and rape are not synonymous. The word has gained in notoriety and lost much of its value through the image it has acquired in the courts of law. Rape refers now almost exclusively to a crime, to an unfair sexual assault of a man against a woman; the message and meaning of its origins in myth remain unheard.

Mothers, maidens and their rapers in myth are not in the first place describing the activities of men, women and children. These are divine beings expressing in metaphor the psychological experience of certain timeless realities. They are not pronouncing moral judgements on whether a form of human behaviour is acceptable, but they are presenting a primordial view of life's patterns. There is much more to the motif of rape than a casual glance might appreciate.

The myth of the rape draws attention to the way the maiden goddess Persephone portrays certain characteristics familiar in human beings. They are qualities which surround Persephone's childlike play, giving an overall impression of innocence. This youthful figure is naive and enthusiastically open to new experience while at the same time being vulnerable, timid, easily hurt and quick to run away; wanting to be taken in adventure yet reluctant to leave the security of home. The nature of the play is clearly not that of athletes intent on breaking records, nor yet is it that of any other artful way of playing at, or playing for, something. There is room for doubt as to whether the maiden understands, or has any idea, what she is playing. Demeter, the mother, may be the one who understands, while Persephone, with a bare minimum of intellectual awareness, is a being who functions with reliance on instinct and a ready wit. The play expresses simply a frame of mind.

For anyone limited to a literal interpretation, the rape of Persephone is an instance of child abuse. Yet, where this image appears in the hymn to Demeter, there is the implication of an event leading, not to destruction, but towards life and life more abundantly. The play is not a game of competition and the rape is not the consequence of play. It is true to say that the order of eternal nature is played and nature is open to seizure by the spirit of death. Persephone playing is like the flowers she picks: a budding flower-like existence, blossoming and opening for a short moment before being plucked and gathered into the underworld abode of death. Her being is play and she is raped, not for purpose, but for being.

As the focus of attention is on the maiden goddess, the motif of death and its significance for hysteria must await a later opportunity for discussion. Suffice it to say that Hades was not the only rapist known to mythology. Many gods of pagan religions follow a similar pattern of behaviour, with pride of place falling to Pan for the persistence with which he chases the fleeing nymphs. Indeed nymphs in this context bear a certain resemblance to Persephone. Without the rape she shares with them an irresistible attractiveness and an elusive ability to disappear before the eyes into the protection of mother nature. But whether as Pan with the nymphs or Hades with Persephone, the spirit of death penetrates a thing of aethereal nature, bringing it body and making it a thing of the senses. In the language of psychology, it brings the substance of true imagination to a natural idea, an incarnation of the spirit.

The contrast of this erotic violence with that in the myth or image of hysteria is very striking. The picture is not that of defloration and union of the 'flower-maiden' with a fertile spirit, but a comparable violence of the mother leaving her maidenhood in sterile isolation. It may sound in some ways like a 'rape of the mother', though it is no rape as such; rather that of a mother and maiden in a situation of mixed sexuality, both taken over by a sinister male spirit. There are no indications that one goddess is less responsible than the other; each of them is highly manipulative in her self-indulgent, unerotic designs. Though the significance is very different, it is understandable that the violence and other features common to both myths might cause them to be mistaken for each other.

The events taking place between the womb and the upper end of the vagina, when understood in terms of myth, bring psychic reality to many different expressions of psychopathology attributed to hysteria. Some of these must now be considered with a view to understanding why hysteria is, and always has been, surrounded by an aura of doubt.

Sex stands out as the theme pressing for attention. It is the feature that has been most prominent throughout the long history of hysteria, starting from the earliest formulations on the womb pathology. Indeed the theme of sex proves to be one of the few consistent threads running throughout the changing face of this protean disease, holding together a medley of events which seem at times to have no logical sequence.

The first recorded account of hysteria is attributed to the Kahun papyrus of ancient Egypt (Veith 1965). It refers to a disorder of woman in which the womb is displaced. The emphasis falls at once on a sexual bias. Some centuries later the writings of Hippocrates and other Greek physicians of the time gave more precise details. They recorded a variety of symptoms accompanying the displacement of the womb, including suffocation, physical contortions and convulsions similar to epileptic fits. It is worthy of note that the seizures, in spite of their similarity, were not taken as epilepsy, in the same way that the myth of the rape is not a literal rape. The cause of the hysteria was the womb wandering around the body as a result of lack of sexual relations with man. In the course of time this deprivation of sex became less a feature of cause and more a symptom of hysteria known as frigidity.

The motif of sex is easy to discern in all references. It was as prominent in the treatment as in the cause of hysteria. The earliest recorded therapy was in the form of compensation for the sexual onesidedness. For example, the suggestion of a male influence appeared in the ancient prescriptions of seductive yet forceful methods used to restore the womb to its natural setting. These and other therapeutic measures supplied the missing male element. In Egypt the dry excrement of man was burned with frankincense to fumigate the patient through the vulva. A related practice invoked the intercession of the male god, Thoth, by burning his waxen image in the likeness of the Ibis bird. This, too, was used for vulval fumigation. Greek medical practice followed a similar pattern, but with the addition of practical advice of a sexual nature. It took the form of counselling widows to remarry and become pregnant through their husbands while, for spinsters, it was considered enough to marry. Though not stated explicitly, the therapeutic measures were in all cases complementary in that they were directed towards correcting the sexual bias of the disease.

The same thread of sex follows through the modified aetiological views of Galen. Sexual abstinence continued to be the important feature though now supplemented in a rather vague way by the hint of a male factor within the woman. Hysteric suffocation was not the product of a wandering womb, but of the infertile retention within the woman's body of secretions thought to bear a resemblance to man's semen. Whether from inside or outside the woman, the absence of a male influence remained essential to the cause. The semen-like secretions may suggest a glimmer of psychological under-standing later to appear as contrasexual components in the works of both Freud and Jung, for Galen's approach to medicine, with his astute observations on the interdependence of mind and body, make him a worthy forerunner of later discoveries in that field.

Striking variations on the theme of sex appeared in mediaeval times. At the time when hysteria was involved with witchcraft and evil spirits, a change took place in the sexual imbalance and its causal role. Emphasis no longer fell on abstinence, but on libertine practices. Woman remained central to the pathology, but her behaviour underwent a problematic change with regard to the male deity; a voluntary compliance with the seductions of the Devil marked her as a witch and a carrier of hysteria. The male influence had become a cause rather than a cure of hysteria; 'suffocation of the mother' had changed its meaning to that of 'suffocation by the witch'.

This pseudo-spiritual phase of its history witnessed an abrupt and surprising swing as the frustration of sexual abstinence gave way to sexual delights with incubi and co-habitation with the Devil. The picture also included the recognition of nymphomania as a symptom of hysteria, an extravagance that extended indirectly to include cases of prostitution and other promiscuity. That swing from abstinence to excessive indulgence marked a surprising and abrupt change in the familiar pattern of hysteria. Nymphomania and other excesses may seem to be out of keeping with the previously understood notion of hysteria, but the change is in fact consistent with the psychology of the myth, as other features of that image will reveal.

The theme of sex in one form or another remained at the forefront of all hysteric disease until comparatively recent times. It began to change in the mid-nineteenth century. France became a centre of work on hysteria, hypnosis and on the pioneering in general of depth psychology at that time. One voice from Paris which spoke with authority against the influence of sex in hysteria was that of the physician, Pierre Briquet (1796–1881). He strongly denied the widely held view that erotic fantasies, desires and frustrations were the central feature of hysteria and stressed rather the importance of hereditary factors, emotional problems and conflicts within the family. Similar thoughts later began to take root and spread in the field of psychiatry, where sex slowly ceased to be considered as a condition of significance. It is a singular coincidence that ceasing to recognise sex in the aetiology was followed soon afterwards by psychiatry ceasing to recognise hysteria as a disease.

This was by no means the only contribution from France. The name of Charcot will always be remembered through a reputation that spread beyond the confines of the medical profession. Charcot was greatly inspired by Briquet, but agreed with him only with reservations that hysteria was not a sexual neurosis. He recognised the strength of the sexual element in his hysteric patients even in the presence of other prominent aetiological factors and did not waver from his opinion that it was of primary importance.

Charcot's train of thought with regard to hysteria was of more inspiration to the psychologists than to the psychiatrists. Freud was prominent amongst those who worked with him and later established his own school of psychology on the foundation of his training as a neurologist and, as would be expected from the pattern of that psychology, the matter of sex remained within hysteria with all the vigour of its early beginnings. Hysteria became a cornerstone in the foundation of psychoanalysis, where the image of frustration from sexual abstinence took on the guise of frustration from sexual repression.

These events are familiar monuments in the history of hysteria and are known to many, though not usually appraised through the perspective of sex. The sequence shows how the theme of sex remained faithful to the psychological evolution of the disease, but grew controversial in the clinical appreciation. This is confirmed by a variety of misleading and contradictory clinical experiences on the contemporary scene. They are to a great extent centred around the symptom of frigidity, widely understood to be one of hysteria's consistent characteristics. Yet far from demonstrating a consistent picture, the evidence of history seems to be saying that almost all or any sexual activities are hysteric. Clearly that cannot be an accurate representation of the facts. It is in itself an exaggeration of an hysteric sort; no more true in fact than to say that all psychopathologies in the pattern of the mother/maiden archetype are hysteric.

What then is the misleading factor in this picture? Whenever the question of deception arises with regard to hysteria, the answer will lie in failing to see the wood for the trees; in failing to see the myth within the scientific undergrowth. The meaning of frigidity is no exception. It has been a symptom of hysteria from the time of the earliest records. The accustomed use of the term implies simply an intense coldness, but, in common parlance, it has come to mean a denial of sex or a lack of sexual heat. Therefore it may come as a surprise to see that hysteric frigidity has little to do with sex in a direct way, for, as already noted, the rejection of sex may take the form of an unerotic refusal or of an equally unerotic nymphomanic extreme of indulgence. The participants in these practices are relatively unimportant and the display, contrary to appearance, holds little erotic attraction or repulsion. Unrelatedness is in fact the mark of hysteria; a well-disguised state of indifference towards the surrounding circumstances. Throughout the centuries sex has in one way or another disguised this particular lack of eroticism.

Such are the salient features of hysteria's frigidity understood through the language of the psyche. Their meaning reaches far beyond instinctive copulation to embrace other models of encounter. The difficulties arising in such meetings are not those of an artless reluctance to *accept* so much as a failure to *recognise* others for what they are worth. Hysteria's quality of unrelatedness is rarely appreciated even though it is extreme both in the cold lack of consideration and in the warmth of theatrical display of the overcompensating disguise. This is the background on which the various sexual encounters are played.

There are several pathological states which, because of sex following patterns common to the two myths, have been associated with, if not identified with, hysteria. By no means all of them are limited to the department of psychological medicine. Any young woman's sexual activities may be made or marred by her mother's interference; but if they are marred, it would be incorrect to assume that the disorder must be hysteria. The motif of mother and maiden appears under many different circumstances of the waking and dreaming life. Its presence in dreams bears testimony to the fact that problems with the mother are limited neither to woman nor to youth, even though youth has the biggest share. The pattern is there for all: the old as well as the young; the neurotic as well as the emotionally stable. With regard to hysteria it may be a matter of considerable difficulty to see where it fits into the picture, especially when signs of contradictory sex practices confuse the picture. They can be as misleading as the ambiguous roles of mother and maiden in the two myths. How can hysteric frigidity embrace both chastity and nymphomania, thus eliminating any simple diagnostic certainty of one or the other?

The answer to this question lies in the theme of the separation that arose earlier while contrasting aspects of the two myths. The theme will arise again; here it is sufficient to draw attention to the *dissociation* that accompanies separation of the protagonists in the hysteric myth. It holds the key to understanding how sexual activities can take place in the presence of a formidable frigidity. Were it not for the dissociation in hysteria, either the continence or the nymphomania would be eliminated, thus simplifying the diagnosis. With it they, like the two mythic participants, mother and maiden, may co-exist; confined to the same body, they can function autonomously with sublime indifference to each other's pursuits. Frigidity and promiscuity are there together.

This archetypal pattern with its hysteric ambiguity may appear as a problem of adolescence in, for example, a young woman's fear of the growing need to give herself in her body to a man, while expressing the equally strong need to deny the impulse and keep that body for herself. It poses the riddle of how to take without being taken. Even the advent of a 'permissive' society has failed to eradicate the archetypal conflict. It is a testing problem to ascertain whether an inexperienced girl is making an erotic advance open to adventure or an hysteric advance with similar appearance, but marked by a search for attention and affection in a performance based on frigidity. The deception strikes as much at the actress as the audience, becoming for her a source of inexplicable frustration and torment of the soul. It may produce various neurotic symptoms, often of serious proportions, with slashing of the skin, burning with cigarettes or mutilation of the flesh in other ways. The syndrome is not in itself hysteria, though it was often vaguely assumed to be so in the past. It may appear in youthful development as a severe neurotic instability or as an episode of a psychotic disruption; but, whatever the presenting picture, an hysteric dissociation merely complicates the scene when it allows nymphomanic practices to take the place of frigid rejection. The encounters may be sexual in effect, though scarcely erotic and they contribute little towards any constructive participation in transformations of the personality appropriate to the time of adolescence.

Another aspect of the same image with the same contradictory circumstances of sexual practices appearing in the presence of frigidity finds its way into the fertility clinics. Barren couples keen to raise a family may not appreciate the strength of unconscious conflict that influences their desires and endeavours. Even after convincing investigations have been carried out to exclude organic causes for the problem, the state of infertility persists as if it were assured by the absence of a womb. For such an obstinate problem, it is surprising that it should often yield with miraculous ease when a child is adopted. Suffice it to say that any hysteric frigidity behind the earnest endeavours of mating lies outside the influence of conscious control, but is correspondingly effective in thwarting the desires. Any realistic attempts at a cure need more than the practicalities of insemination, for there is clearly a complex at work responsible for the state that only seems to be infertile; a complex behind an attitude that has some bearing on the psychic image of maiden, mother and rape.

As one would expect under any circumstances where the archetypal world of sex is prominent, both male and female homosexuality may claim a place of importance in the picture of hysteria. Especially as a collective phenomenon, it is open to infection by the extravagant emotionality of hysteria that can imbue it with a greater significance than it warrants.

Homosexuality covers a wide spectrum, reaching from its presence as a natural feature of the human personality to its appearance in the field of medicine as a pathology of relatedness. The social implications have long been a controversial subject of discussion, particularly in the realms of the law, religion and medicine; but here it is of concern only to the extent that it meets hysteria and the pathological implications that arise. Needless to say, the whole spectrum of homosexuality is susceptible. The extremes of the spectrum may be comparatively rare to encounter, but there is a large area in the centre with poorly defined boundaries where the deceptive ways of hysteria need attention. For the phenomenon referred to as homosexuality by the media and public is to a large extent a one-sided exaggeration of bisexuality. Few would deny that the extravagant demonstrations have been, and still are, to some extent necessary in order to contend with long-lasting moralistic prejudice shown towards all forms of homoeroticism. It threatens to become problematic only when hysteria manipulates the situation into appearing more than it really is and blinds participants to the significance of their sexuality. Indeed the problem – recently exaggerated by the advent of permissiveness in matters of sex – often lies more in sexuality than in homosexuality, bringing unhelpful and unnecessary hazards to jeopardize the gay movement.

Taking part in the same cultural scene, transvestite practices show certain similar features. They, too, are readily prone to hysteria, but here it is not so much a matter of appearing as something it is not, as of its popular entertainment value that spreads on a wave of emotion like an hysteric infection and catches the impressionable individual. To the extent that it is a phenomenon of culture, it appears rather like a 'fashion'; though, unlike the more truly cultural phenomena as in, for example, clothing fashions, transvesticism catches only the highly impressionable.

These few examples, taken from a wide choice, are enough to show that sex in hysteria is not always what it seems to be. Not the sexuality itself, but the attitude in which it is practised, defines the nature of the hysteric participation. The point needs stating, for it is open to misunderstanding. The firm impression from the works of writers, both ancient and modern, is that hysteria presents in the first place as a sexual disease. Especially in the recent psychological phase of its history, hysteria has been overburdened with sex and its sufferers assumed to be obsessed with sexual fantasies as the source of their troubles. But such is far from the case; that impression is itself an hysteric exaggeration. Sex and frigidity have always been present with hysteria. Any form of sexual practices may take place, but the attitude which accompanies them is such that they are distinguished by an erotic deficiency. That is the feature marking them as hysteria.

It seems that any consideraton of hysteria means an encounter with ambiguity and with an inherent difficulty in reading the situation. The hazards are not limited to clinical experiences; even mythology falls under the spell of deception, as in the case of the inappropriate name, the *Hysteria*, given to an ancient ritual practice in honour of the mother goddess. The feast was dedicated, not to the threefold goddess, but to Aphrodite at Argos. It was the custom during these celebrations for young pigs to be thrown into a pit dug in the earth, attended by women dressed as men and men as women wearing veils. The sexual allegories of the ritual are apparent and there is surely a close association between the name, hysteria, and the fertilising of a womb as a pit dug in the earth. Yet the feature most likely to catch the imagination as hysteria is not the pit, but the mixture of the sexes, the exhibition of the transvestites. In all probability some degree of hysteria was present amongst the participants; but a careful reading of the image shows that, in spite of the emotional extravagances and theatrical appearances, this was not a festival of hysteria. The picture it presents is, if anything, closer to a reversal of order, as in the carnival to reverence the raving god, Dionysos. Indeed, hysteria has also been attributed to Dionysos on account of the bisexual nature of that god; the maenads, his raving women followers, are claimed as the image of hysteric woman. In fact the maenads, belonging to the image of Dionysos, are no more representative of hysteria than is the feast at Argos in reverence to Aphrodite. The image in both celebrations hints more towards a union of opposites than an hysteric dissociation.

Reminiscent of the feast of the *Hysteria*, but also suggestive of the poor differentiation of the goddesses in the myth of hysteria, is the way the sexes in contemporary culture have lost their accustomed sexual identity. Unisex is the vogue. It appears in many different forms, not limited to that of the current fashion in clothing. The distribution of domestic duties, and even the ordination of either sex to the priesthood in some religious communities, are also manifestations of the unisex pattern. These examples catch the attention and raise questions, though their significance goes far beyond any heated arguments of whether they are to be judged right or wrong. The hysteric image fills unisex with the ominous presence of a deception which suggests that woman is really the same as man and man as woman, thus abolishing one of life's most prominent and meaningful polarities. Social barriers as well as social structures have collapsed and boundaries are rarely recognised, let alone respected. This is the unstable shadow side of unisex in the culture, and it is deceptive. There can surely be no good reason why domestic duties, style of clothing, patterns of employment, sports or any other aspects of the daily scene should not be shared by both sexes. The question is, in what manner does the motivation arrive?

Those familiar with the psychology of C. G. Jung will appreciate that there is an association between unisex and the role of the hermaphrodite in the psychology of alchemy, though precisely what relationship they bear to each other is not plain to see. The alchemical *opus* takes its origin in the unity of wholeness of the *prima materia*. The pattern of the *opus* leads from there to separation of the *materia* and so to the alchemical hermaphrodite as the ultimate union of oppposites. The hermaphrodite is in fact the Stone, the *lapis philosophorum*, never quite achieved in this lifetime.

The great majority of people are unaware of androgeny or the hermaphrodite and the role this image plays in cultural expressions. Correspondingly, the achievements of a unisex culture are hardly to be compared with those of the *opus*. But in the context of this work, unisex – as with other patterns of sex – is of importance only in so far as it meets with hysteria, for that is where deception may catch it on a crest of enthusiasm making unisex seem more than it is. To put this another way, the meaning behind the alchemical hermaphrodite, born of the tension of opposites, is a move towards self-knowledge. Unisex falls far short of this pattern. In practice it makes its appearance to a large extent not from tension, but from a collapse between masculine and feminine poles making a pseudohermaphrodite: a contamination of psychic opposites giving rise to an undifferentiated mixture of characteristics. Extravagant demonstrations of unisex, both public and private, are for the most part theatrical displays of self-indulgence rather than milestones on the way to self-knowledge. Together with these activities, speculative thoughts spring readily to mind, thoughts which are both seductive and suggestive: are men and women perhaps really the same? Does it really matter who is father in the house and who is mother? Does it really matter if there is a home? If, as is often the case with such speculations, there follows some surrender of responsibility for the children, it means for the parental consciousness a backward move towards childhood. The same effect creeps into responsibility towards society where it is important to remember that the significance of 'back towards childhood' lies in symbolic meaning of returning to a primitive level of functioning. It encourages an hedonistic society relatively unconscious of what it is doing; not that primitive means hedonistic, but once the seductions of a sophisticated society have reached individual or collective awareness, it is difficult to abandon them, and their indulgence will be served by a repressed consciousness.

Unisex may not knowingly aspire to the heights of alchemy, but that is not to say its practices are in themselves destructive. The hazardous risk is an hysteric deception that tends to get in the way and carry unisex away from its slender roots in the alchemical hermaphrodite. Hysteria may inspire it with enthusiasm, but at the expense of meaning.

One of the most important changes to take place in the history of hysteria has been the recent decision of the medical profession no longer to recognise it as a specific unit of illness in its own right. This forthright decision, made with the authority of physicians, has brought in its wake the naive assumption that hysteria no longer exists. Hysteria, needless to say, remains unaltered. Physicians have, rightly or wrongly, denied it the status of a disease, but hysteria continues as before to influence both individual and collective patterns of behaviour. One feature of this influence suggesting itself to the imagination is the striking coincidence that the move to deny hysteria appeared with the beginnings of a sexually permissive and increasingly hysteric society. For society, too, reflects the dominance of a mythic background. Fashions of all sorts bear witness to the phenomenon, and hysteric frigidity in an exaggeratedly 'get together' society is the prominent example.

Permissiveness is ready to appear wherever there is the lack of a firm structure; at the same time structures begin to disappear when boundaries are unrecognised. In other words, the dimmed border-lines of hysteria make it an ideal setting for permissiveness to thrive. This is not always limited to sex. The present obsessive drive to group activities of all sorts reflects hysteric qualities and appearances which, like those of permissive sex, are not always simply what they seem to be. In many so-called group activities those participants infected with hysteria touch on the shadow side and limit it to a relatively unconscious mass phenomenon. Without altering the pattern of events, the hysteria brings emotion in plenty with excitement, mis-placed exaggeration and a suspicion of insincerity. The desire to form groups may be compensating for the threat of loneliness in an over-populated world, but the presence of hysteric indifference in rela-tionships detracts from the purpose of those groups; their achieve-ments are not always as satisfactory as they appear.

Following the same pattern of unrecognised boundaries are the reactions of many people to a fear of total destruction through detergents, pesticides, pollution and even nuclear weapons. They hold a similar misrepresentation of the circumstances. The dangers are very real indeed, yet the significant factor in this context is that the accompanying hysteria exaggerates in an unrelated manner without respecting those dangers. An hysteric anxiety rather than an instinctive fear dominates the scene. It blinds its victims to the element of necessity in the phenomena. In this way there is a loud cry and exaggerated activity aimed at eliminating the fear, but with a failure to appreciate the fuller significance of the cultural situation.

There can be no doubt that the theme of sex is prominent in the way it runs through the history of hysteria. It has at all times been recognised as a feature of the disease, even though the extreme changes in its presentation have to a large extent taken place without conscious awareness. Close attention to the background myth of hysteria brings the satisfaction, not only of confirmation, but of meaning to the situation. The insights it carries are often surprising; none more so than those from the contemporary permissive scene.

Even before the decision of medical authority not to recognise hysteria, the incidence of individual cases was on the wane. Mass hysteria, on the other hand, both as acute outbreaks and as more chronic, collective developments is, if not on the increase, at least constant. It is especially noticeable in expressions of unisex and of sexual permissiveness which between them have intensified rather than remedied many problems of sexuality. These two phenomena are characteristic representations in the culture of a society often referred to unconvincingly as manic. It may be nearer the truth to say that society is hysteric. Certainly there are many indications that the over-enthusiastic, extroverted demonstrations are not always what they seem to be, and amongst them unisex and permissiveness are outstanding in the way they abound as an exaggerated compensation for failure to recognise hysteria.

5

SUFFOCATING RELATIONS

The physicians of ancient times who wrote on hysteria may have been concerned with the sexuality of their subject, yet these same physicians were describing clinically a form of suffocation. They called it the 'suffocation of the mother'. The records leave no doubt that both sex and suffocation are central to hysteric disease.

In view of the frequency with which the term suffocation appears, it may come as a surprise to realise how little serious attention it has received in comparison with other features of hysteria. Clinical details have been discussed in plenty through generations of medical study and yet the significance of suffocation passes relatively unnoticed; like sex, it has to a great extent been taken for granted. How can it be that these two basic characteristics of hysteria have for so long forfeited priority of attention to lesser features? Is suffocation really the powerful pivot of hysteria it seems to be? Certainly the evidence of the myth as well as the symptomatology would answer unhesitatingly: yes, it is.

The question of why the subjects of hysteria experience asphyxia has accumulated its share of theories and explanations. Many of them would be largely meaningless were it not for the metaphor of air and the association between this and asphyxia. For the significance of this simple physiology reaches beyond the mechanics of respiration to include the wider meaning of spirit in the symbol of air. Nowhere is this better represented than by the spontaneous movement of a wind that ripples the waters: an invisible, autonomous

43

force reflected in the movement of inert matter. Spirit is the source of inspiration and, like air, is breathtaking in all senses of the word. Suffocation is the inevitable consequence if it is in short supply; but to a certain extent this also results when the supply is excessive. In other words, spirit can be suffocating in excess in the same way that a high wind inhibits breathing.

Understood in these terms, the clinical picture suggests that the spirit of hysteria is a suffocating spirit. On the other hand, whether the myth it reflects indicates suffocation in deficiency or excess remains to be seen. Certainly there is strong emphasis on the presence of suffocation in hysteria. To quote again the concise description in the 'Timaeus' of Plato, 'the womb . . . distressed and disturbed, straying about the body and cutting off the passages of the breath, impedes respiration'. This can only mean that the origins of hysteria lie in a dissociation of the mother and that the dissociation is also, as Plato implies, a form of asphyxia.

The term 'suffocation' implies a state of respiratory embarrass-ment often accompanied by choking. Causes of this distress are legion and they are all based on the same pattern of biological changes resulting from altered gaseous exchanges. It means that the nature of the suffocation in dental anaesthesia, for example, differs not at all from that of infantile paralysis of the respiratory muscles. Physical distress in all cases may fluctuate from a harmless dis-comfort to an immediate threat to life. The question is whether the asphyxia of these and similar suffocating pathologies is the same as that known as 'hysteric suffocation'.

Comment has been made on the readiness with which hysteria changes its features to suit the culture of the moment. Hysteric suffocation proves to be no exception, and its changing explanations tell the tale. Hippocrates in about the early fourth century BC, and others before him, described the suffocation of the mother. Soranus, a famous physician of the same period, used a less rich language for the same condition which he described as a fit accompanied by respiratory obstruction together with aphonia and a seizure of the senses. Although in his opinion the womb did not wander from its site in the pelvis, it was nevertheless responsible for the seizure. These physicians, each in his own way, were describing suffocation in the wind pipe by the *globus hystericus*, the classic symptom whose name, like that of hysteria itself, is attributed to Hippocrates. The same symptom with the same name is still recognised in medical practice, albeit with a markedly different explanation of the pathology.

The *globus hystericus* defines the sensation of a suffocating, choking lump in the throat, assumed to be the result of a wandering womb lodged in the upper thorax. Centuries later this was explained as a neurosis of the pharynx with contraction of its muscle tissue. But between these widely differing aetiologies, there were others. Mediaeval thought on hysteria was influenced by the theme of witchery and it attributed this same condition to the Devil inserting balls of obstruction into the windpipe. The early neurologists described this as a spasm of the glottis accompanying fits which originated in the head. Later generations understood hysteric suffocation as an attack of the 'vapours' or similar vegetative upset, but their ideas tended more towards suffocation as a subjective sensation than to an organic disorder. There are descriptions in plenty of suffocation occurring in particular locations of the body and in specific organs as a result of the wandering womb coming to rest in those foreign parts; the leading, but not the only, example was the *globus hystericus*. That does not complete the picture; suffocation was also described in the womb itself. With this location a note of uncertainty enters, for there is ambiguity in the name 'suffocation of the mother'. As with the theme of rape and violence, the same question arises: is the mother the active or the passive participant? Does the womb suffocate the body or vice versa? Some light on these problems may be gained from a contrast of the hysteric image with that of the mother beyond the boundaries of hysteria.

A moral to deduce from the myth of Eleusis is that there are times for a mother and her maiden to be together and times when it is essential that they separate. This is a simple maxim of behaviour, yet an archetypal reality neglected with surprising regularity in everyday life. The consequences, if not always pathological, are to say the least turbulent, as any other members of the family are well aware. But when heard in terms of the mythology of the soul, the meaning of this simple maxim lies hidden in features of the separation hinted at in a previous section. In the myth told by Homer, the separation of mother and maiden is effectively achieved by the entrance of a male spirit as the god, Pluto, taking possession of his bride. In that told by Hippocrates, the image is again of separation, but of a different order. Here, it is not that of a maiden abducted from the mother, but of the two torn apart in a setting where the natural order determines eternal togetherness. Both procedures are violent, but their consequences differ widely.

Hysteria tells its myth in the language of physiology rather than in that of a theology appropriate to Eleusis. The image implies that the womb, the continuation of the vagina, is displaced into the body cavity where it resembles a free agent separated from its moorings in the pelvis. That impression of separation is deceiving. The wandering of the mother is not the clean break it seems to be. Womb and vagina are naturally inseparable, meaning that the displacement in hysteria is not a physical parting, but a form of togetherness stretched to its limits. A sharp rise of tension is the inevitable outcome of the two components intent on moving apart. The pattern is in ways comparable, but not identical, to the familiar gynaeco-logical disorders of retroversion and prolapse uteri, where contact is maintained with the moorings. The significant difference is that retroversion and prolapse are for the most part downward dis-placements with myth suggests that the direction in hysteria is upwards and is extreme.

Wandering the body cavity in hysteria implies a mother and maiden wilfully striving to avoid each other while obliged to remain together in an uncooperative bondage. In other words, the in-discriminate wanderings do not refer to separation as division but, as mentioned previously, to separation as a *dissociation*; the auto-nomous functioning within the same body structure of two char-acters having no regard for each other. As C. G. Jung once wrote, 'the hysterical disposition means the opposites inherent in every psyche are further apart than in normal people' (1964, p. 423). The myth and the vivid impression of tension confirms it. There is an atmosphere of oppression. This is no restless search for a lost maiden, but a contemptuous spread of discount and disease born of suffocating frustration.

Turning now to Homer's more explicit account of the mother, it becomes clear that the rape involves yet another aspect of separation; yet once again there is no real division. Rape in this context does not, as might be assumed, divide an archetypye, but adds a dimension to the togetherness of mother and maiden. For separation here means, not division, but *differentiation*. Mother and maiden represent central components of feminity which require differentiation for the human being, and for this undertaking the role of the male spirit is indispensable. Hysteria is the reflection of a situation wherein this differentiation of mother and maiden does not take place. It is as if these two prominent psychic components are choked on spirit; there is no healthy inbreak of spirit from outside, but an excess of suffocating animosity from inside.

In the field of medical pathology, hysteria is well known to possess the characteristics of deception and mistaken identity. The reference to undifferentiated feminity and the suffocating animosity extends that field into complex areas of psychopathology. It raises a question for the psychotherapist whether the myth of hysteria is no more an example of the suffocation known to students of C. G. Jung's psychology as a neurotic state of undifferentiated animus. There are indeed good grounds for assuming that an overt appearance of hysteria is similar to the state of animus that leads to neurosis. It would imply that hysteria is only a neurotic problem of individuation when in fact hysteria's role in individuation, as a later section of this work will confirm, is precisely not that of neurosis. Any theatrical and emotional outburst that holds stubbornly to an opinion is not necessarily the blind fixaton of a neurosis, though it is certainly a demonstation of animosity and may be hysteric. As with any other psychic component, animus, whether prominent or in the background, is always present; but here it is not relevant to the image. With regard to suffocation, hysteria speaks of other features. This much is clear: the presence of hysteria with its highly emotional and

47

stifling atmosphere of undifferentiated, mixed identities is a form of demonstration. The image in the demonstration is that of a maiden who cannot play, for she has become an understanding, controlling mother and, correspondingly, a mother who cannot understand, for she is in the state of an overexcited, but ignorant child. Suffocation, though picked up quickly by the hysteric subject, is also infectious and picked up to some degree by all those in the vicinity.

Is it the rape or the hysteria that brings the surprise? That the image of overpowering a maiden by rape could represent relief rather than an intensification of the asphyxia may sound absurd to the unimaginative reader; yet relief through differentiation is none the less exactly the meaning it holds in this context. Pluto ploughing through the material earth, separating and freeing, is a forced inspiration at a moment when suffocation is imminent. In spite of appearances, this necessary violence does not take place in hysteria.

Myth is the very essence of psychological life and its locution is everywhere and at all times expressing patterns both in and outside conscious awareness. The purest representative for the individual is the dream, the experience closest to the source and offering the clearest examples of collective mythic patterns participating in and forming the myths of individual lives. One such example is the following dream from a patient with pronounced hysteric characteristics. Any personal enlightenments it may have brought to the awareness of the patient are in this instance of less importance than the illustration it provides for hysteric suffocation in general:

> 'On opening a cupboard, I found myself looking at a young girl who had been observing me through the keyhole. She started to tell me about her life, chatting unselfconsciously. Suddenly her mother came in and the atmosphere became very stiff and hostile. She told the child to have nothing to do with me.'

Of particular relevance to the theme of hysteria is the fact that the dreamer suffered from various emotional forms of suffocation, one of which took the form of a fear of schizophrenia. Does the dream address this fear? Dreams are not, and do not make, diagnoses, and this dream is no exception, though it does point the way towards features of hysteria while saying nothing about schizophrenia. For opening the cupboard is confrontation with, among other things, a suffocation of the mother. It says that, when the dreamer discovers a maiden in the cupboard, the mother enters and the spontaneity of play and the joy of living disappear into a stiff, hostile atmosphere. The discovery is that of a calculated oppression in a situation 'raped', as it were, or seized by a mother, but not inspired by a male counterpart. Furthermore, the dream tells how tension rises as play is excluded, meaning that the refreshing openness and receptivity of youth are lost to rigid disapproval; spontaneity is replaced by calculated pose. An enchanting 'breathless expectancy' of a maiden turns into a suffocating dominance of a mother.

A first glance at this dream seems to imply that the disturbing influence is the mother. In the context of hysteria this would mean that the mother is the cause. But is she? Is this drama only a crushing correction from a mother, or is a touchy child intent on having its way in some outrageous prank? Perhaps both patterns are to some extent relevant. The dream is not speaking of cause or blame, and its communication will be misunderstood if some attempt is not made to avoid the psychological prejudice that invariably (and often hysterically) overestimates everything to do with 'mother'.

It is understandable that, for anyone who cannot see beyond the physical shortcomings of human childhood and the limits they impose in an adult world, the so-called mother will seem to wield the greater power. But in a situation where myth is the primary concern, as, for example, in the formulation of the dream, the psychological reality must modify that assumption. The mythic background tells another tale; its significance for the patient is far greater than that of a disciplinary mother. It raises a question: why should there be this exaggerated supremacy of the mother when the mythology of the maiden is of no less significance? These are divinities and not actual human beings, adult or child. They do not need to vie with each other for supremacy, for the maiden is equal to the mother. Witness the awesome presence in the underworld where stands the same daughter of Demeter who was raped while playing. The eyes of a developmental psychologist may see only a girl not yet grown to adulthood and miss the majesty of the maiden Persephone, wife of Hades, not *becoming* a mother, but *being* a maiden. There is more to Persephone than a dutiful, subservient daughter. In other words, archetypal dominance is easily misplaced; there is an error in assuming that the power lies wholly with the 'older' woman. From that premise it is but a step to falling into the folly of the psycho-therapist who blames the parent for the patient's neurosis while overlooking the majestic power of the individual personality, how-ever youthful the patient may be.

The pattern of the dream presents many features of the hysteric myth and, if met without prejudice, it affirms that the mother is not the sole offender. Oppression is in the atmosphere. Both women are essential to it and the one is no less formidable in its role than the other. The psychological predicament expressed in terms of the myth is one of a mixed identity of characters in need of diff-erentiation. Suffocating effects are mutual.

The centre which directs the oppressive atmosphere of an hysteric suffocation is play. If one stops to consider how much caprice, eccentricity and theatrical superficiality have appeared in hysteria, it comes as a surprise to realise the extent of the underlying earnest intent and serious manner. Hysteria is no light-hearted state of being. In that violent encounter between mother and maiden there is no fun, whatever the clinical outcome may be; at every turning it lacks play. Yet there is contradiction, or seeming contradiction, in that observation. It may lack the element of play, but is itself considered to be essentially a form of play, a theatrical performance or a role played to achieve some gain. Play turns out to be the instrument for one of hysteria's deceptive appearances. This feature of the disease may not claim the age-old prominence of sex or suffocation, but it is none the less of central importance, especially since the emphasis placed on hysteria's theatrical characteristics.

There is no doubt that play is markedly absent in the myth of hysteria. If it is present in any form it can only be in the dark recesses of that myth where it cannot be seen and is likely to take a sinister turn. Yet that absence set beside the image of the Eleusis myth draws attention to the motif of play and to its meaning. It warrants a close consideration, not only in the interests of play in general, but in particular in the interests of the light it throws on hysteria.

Play is a popular subject for discussion, especially in the field of psychotherapy where descriptions abound and the roles of players are explained. Many different purposeful uses are attributed to play: that it is a necessary training for the young to prepare for the more serious work of life; that it is an effective way to get rid of excessive energy; that it cultivates restraint; that it is a form of wish fulfilment; that it fulfils a need for relaxation. They are all true to some extent, yet say little about the nature of play itself. That information requires the authority of its origins in some fundamental, archetypal expression as, for instance, in a god or goddess of play. But no divinity obliges with an answer to that call. Can it mean that there is no play within the godhead and no reflection in the psyche? Certainly not. If, as Shakespeare says, 'all the world's a stage' on which people play their parts, that is in itself but a reflection of the theatre in the human soul wherein are plays, audience and stage. Here the god-images in varied disguises make their exits and their entrances; here they make up in the dressing rooms, play and withdraw. In the historic setting of a human life they are experienced as appearing in materials woven from the world of human beings with which they play out the movements of imagination. Beyond that existence nothing is known of the gods.

It is often said that play is the lifestyle of the gods. Apollo plays his lute and Hermes plays his tricks, just as Eros is the model of love play. Others have their particular characteristics of play, but Persephone has one special feature in that, amongst all her other attributes, she just plays. This does not mean that Persephone is essentially the goddess of play, but that she is, more than any other of that Pantheon, the divinity telling specifically about play rather than about playing something. From all accounts Persephone likes to play and must play to fulfil her being. In what material woven from human existence has she clothed herself to play the part of playing?

As recounted by Persephone herself in the hymn to Demeter, she was with the daughters of Okeanos playing in a lovely meadow, gathering a variety of different flowers all mixed together. This is indeed an artless pastime appropriate to a naive thing of nature, a child of innocence of whom Homer says, 'its brightness is wonderful'. That image emanates youthful, unconscious being. One could imagine that Persephone is hardly aware of what she is doing; her mind cannot be said to be on flower-gathering with any serious deliberation. Here she is showing anything but that purpose and understanding which might be attributed to the mother, Demeter.

The *Kore* in a meadow amongst the children and flowers surely contributes to the idea of play being an activity of the very young, if not the prerogative of children. Yet this must be an unnecessarily narrow appreciation in view of the fact that adults – mature adults at that – play as well as, and in some ways as much as, children. Even animals are not dependent on human beings for an introduction to play; young and old, they, too, possess the potential. To a greater or lesser degree, play belongs to us all. If much that is said about play is, from a psychological point of view, vaguely unsatisfying, it is to some extent because of the misapprehension that it really belongs to children. In this way play as a psychic factor is overlooked or, in other words, not appreciated as an *attitude*. Play in terms of human kind is a *Kore* attitude, a way of seeing and not simply a purposeful activity called play.

The picture of a maiden playing in a meadow is inseparable from the idea of fun. In fact it may be said that fun is the foremost characteristic of all that Persephone holds with regard to play. It belongs within the meaning of the word that, if fun is no longer present, play ceases to be. This singular quality of merriment goes far towards explaining why the spoil-sport is the recipient of such severe censure and, too, why hysteria arouses such antagonism and disapproval. The ready assumption is that the cheat is the offender who receives the stronger censorship as the unforgiveable sinner, though in reality it is the spoil-sport who causes the greater offence. Moral indignation distorts the picture and disguises the fact that cheating is not incompatible with play. Though morally undesirable, it may still be, and can still maintain, fun. Only when in the service of the spoil-sport does it become totally unacceptable, for the intervention of the spoil-sport is more than the simple spoiling of a game. Not only are rules ignored, but the whole order of play is violated. The play attitude has vanished with the profane inbreak of a serious and wilful deliberation, of a purposeful calculation that dominates to the exclusion of fun.

Let the profane inbreak stand as a reminder not to overlook the spiritual or sacred aspect of what takes place. Disinterest is a quality on which the attitude of play thrives; it defines a state of detachment and calls to mind the counsel of countless religious directors. Spiritually these features serve the interests of becoming more human and, at the same time, the attitude of play. Disinterest – in sharp contrast to uninterest – is a selfless way of involvement, open and receptive and without calculated purpose or gain. It stands apart from the familiar wants and appetites that call for immediate gratification; disinterest may in fact interrupt the demands of appetite. In this way the attitude of play has an important place in the regulation of instinctive and compulsive behaviour. Its absence in hysteria means that play is only half real. Here the profanity is strong; there is purpose and gain in its apparently meaningless manipulations. In hysteria the play is that of playing at, or for, something as in role playing and theatrical demonstration without disinterested involvement. Persephone is seized in mythology by an underworld spirit; but in hysteria the absence of the play attitude brings a different form of seizure with suffocation.

Mistaken identity has been a consistent characteristic of hysteria at every turn in its history. Needless to add, it persists even in the face of the decision not to recognise hysteria as an individual disease. The outcome of this proclivity to false identity is that hysteria has been identified with a number of different medical syndromes, yet has failed to identify itself as an illness with any conviction. The record it presents cannot but cast doubt on its authenticity and must ultimately raise the question, what is the nature of hysteria and what position does it hold in medical practice if not that of a disease? It has already been said, and may be repeated with a confidence gained by contrasting the myths, that hysteria in the field of pathology is not what it seems to be. As an illness it differs from other illnesses in the same way that the *globus hystericus* differs from other forms of asphyxia. That is to say, hysteric suffocation, in contrast to that of emphysema or infantile paralysis, is organically impossible, limited in effect and never immediately dangerous to life. Yet there is need for further clarification. Muscular contractions in various parts of the body, including the muscles of respiration, have always figured highly in descriptions of hysteria. Tetanic spasms, for example, and contortions amounting even to opisthotonos – the phenomenon of suspending the body weight on the head and heels only – are sensational features of hysteria particularly prevalent in the nineteenth century, and to that extent some physical asphyxia must accompany that degree of disorder. Nevertheless asphyxia, seen purely from the point of view of hysteria, is relatively unimportant beside the subjective impression of suffocation expressing the real nature of the disorder in which affect is out of all proportion to the physical cause.

Hysteria is indeed not what it seems to be and it causes mistakes of identity because of the astonishing potential for mimicry enacted with a skill beyond the expectations of the most accomplished actor. The adopted role is played with great conviction. Though not in itself a disease, it bears the same close kinship with the disease it mimics as that between the two related myths of Eleusis and hysteria. The artistry of hysteria is itself a living and effective force: suggestive, infectious and transforming. On that account it is possible to witness hysteria actually becoming the disease it mimics, as when the convulsions become true epilepsy or the organic symptoms evolve into a psychosomatic disorder. The muscular contractions in the strangulation of the womb, often mentioned by earlier authors, prove not to be those of a gynaecological illness, but an expression of the suffocation of the mother. Nevertheless the hysteric attitude it defines can, and often does, precipitate a true organic disorder. This may be observed in recent times in the attitude that blackens woman's menstruation by calling it 'the curse'. It holds an hysteric element that fosters disease. The logic of this insult may be understandable in the light of the tempo and tension in modern living, but the meaning is clear and sinister: where there is rejection of woman's most womanly characteristic there can be little place for woman herself. The hysteria in that morbid attitude sets in motion a process moving through functional complaints of the uterus to the appearance of dysmenorrhoea, a syndrome that has now established a place in the field of psychosomatic medicine. But at the same time the movement is not necessarily towards morbidity. Whatever disease may manifest in the presence of hysteric mimicry, the hysteria is not the disease itself. Transformation in the direction of health may equally well follow the theatrical enactment.

Hysteria is described as a disease, but not without reservations. The nature of its unlikely, enigmatic involvement with other diseases, together with other notable features of its history, such as the pleasurable indulgences and their diabolic consequences of suffering and torture and execution, the involvement in mediaeval times in legal and ecclesiastical disputes and the whole gamut of emotional excesses, suggests that hysteria is something *more* than is understood by the word 'illness'.

As a disease, hysteria has claimed a mammoth share of attention. On the other hand, as a factor in some way participating in the transformation of people and the times they live in, it is ignored. Hysteria, as a mover of culture, warrants more serious attention than it has received. The changing clinical appearances may be open to suspicion, but the manner of involvement in each enterprise has always been more than pure chance or mistaken diagnosis. Early scientific medicine grew under the influence of hysteric uncertainty; religious beliefs and mysticism changed and matured with hysteria to the forefront, both in and outside the monastery; its role in the differentiation of neurosis during the eighteenth and nineteenth centuries has been no less significant. It may seem as if hysteria has now been eliminated, but it would be truer to say that its role is slowly gaining recognition as not being one of orthodox illness.

6

A BURNING QUESTION

In the preceding essays on sexuality and suffocation some relatively clear aspects of the mother and maiden in the myth of hysteria were touched upon. Other aspects of this same myth are less clearly represented, though by no means less important. Indeed, in the light of discussion, it may prove that they will be judged the more important.

Obscurity is a prominent characteristic of hysteria and, by its very nature, the disease is far from consistent or implicit in all its appearances. There are good grounds for suspecting that obscurity is a reflection of its origins, for a similar quality lies in the way the myth harbours hidden features. Let it not be forgotten that the myth of hysteria is a tale of Mediterranean origins about the mythology of the great threefold goddess of ancient Greece. The exposition is clear, but reserved; it tells of the mother in relation to the maiden in such a manner that it conceals the threefold nature of the image. The reserve is also present in the way the subjects of hysteria deceive without quite being guilty of deliberate deception. The disease itself uses the obscurity inherent in its nature to further that effect. A suggestion of this has already appeared in the motif of rape, which is clearly defined in one myth while a similar violence is at the same time, though not mentioned, categorically denied by the other. A shadow is cast over this area and the cause is not hard to locate in the threefold goddess.

There are surely few people who have never heard tell of the rape of Persephone. For those more closely acquainted with the events the name is coupled with that of Demeter, whose presence cannot be excluded without reducing the mythologem to a meaningless violence. But that is not all. For many it may come as a surprise to learn that a third divinity, the moon goddess Hecate, plays a part of equal importance in the dramatic abduction. Her activities are unobtrusive and the name in this setting is rarely remembered except by those, comparatively few, who may have more than a passing interest in the plot. Together, the three female characters are the great threefold goddess and, separately, each plays an equally vital role in the rape. It should not be necessary to add of this trinity that, though individual in nature, each is an aspect of the others. They carry between them the highest authority in the realms of under-world, earth and sky.

Hecate's unobtrusiveness is a detail not to be underrated in the study of hysteria. Why should this divine presence, prominent in many other situations, pass almost unnoticed here where her role is of no greater or lesser importance than those of Demeter and Persephone? What lies behind the modest participation in the dim recesses of this drama? There must be a wealth of wisdom prompting this light-bearing divinity to take a place of relative obscurity. Some prominent features of the threefold goddess in relation to hysteria have already emerged from contrasting the two myths, but any contribution from the singular characteristics of Hecate was not amongst them. That omission must now be made good.

Even in the myth of Eleusis, the features of Hecate are relatively obscure, but there is at least mention of her presence. In the myth of hysteria, the obscurity is increased to extreme darkness. Here the name, Hecate, does not receive so much as an indirect mention, though none the less present in the threefold nature of the goddess image. It would be easy, but quite incorrect, to assume that Hecate's presence is irrelevant to hysteric disorder.

A lack of prominence is no indication of a minor role. In this instance it signifies remoteness rather than unimportance. The name Hecate itself refers to distance. It identifies an outstanding figure distinguished by a bright headdress appropriate to a 'bringer of light'. That it should be deemed outstanding has a faint ring of contradiction in that Hecate is at the same time a dark goddess and indistinct. The dark moon, the mirror of time, is her special prerogative, her dealings sinister and touched with an ancient magic. Not even the achievements of space travel have succeeded yet in dispelling the threat of uncertainty that lies on the border of the crescent moon where the supernatural powers of the night mingle with witchery and sorcery. The mysterious presence has a similar menacing uncertainty on the borders of the underworld where, according to Hesiod, the same goddess may be found leading a nightly swarm of ghosts in the company of barking dogs. Dark, distant and indistinct borders are her domain; but the nature of that borderline existence can only be assessed in terms of close association with the other two aspects of the threefold goddess.

One special feature of those distant borders, stamping them with the seal of the threefold goddess, is their shadowy relation to time in its different dimensions. There is mythic expression of this in the reciprocity of the mother and her maiden, who, together, give a faint suggestion of eternity in the way they represent an unceasing cycle with each fulfilling an individual destiny yet sooner or later returning to union with the other. It is a puzzling theme; were the mother and maiden ever really separate or merely spinning the illusion of life that makes them seem apart? The nature of their interplay seems to ignore death. It differs fundamentally in meaning from that of the father and the boy, wherein myth decrees that the one must die before the other can reign alone until death. To confuse the male and female destinies were a sorry misunderstanding.

Hecate lends the uncanny atmosphere of the dark moon to this dimension of time. The contribution has unpredictable consequences; but, whether exciting, distressing or downright terrfying, it is effective in the way it anchors the experience of time in another reality, moving it, as it were, from philosophic speculation to psychological experience. Hecate not only breathes a whiff of eternity into an indisputably finite world, but at the same time charges it with magic and superstition. Coincidence suddenly takes on a numinous quality often disconcerting to the point of madness;

not necessarily insanity, but madness. The riddle of the chicken and the egg must be taken seriously, for the young and the old are no longer a beginning and an end, but have become two aspects of a psychic experience. Time becomes a source of uncertainty and misunderstanding.

On closer inspection it threatens to become an even more disconcerting problem and raises difficult questions on the attitude adults as a whole may adopt towards youth; on the way parents may behave towards their children. Old and young are not simply superior and inferior in age. A psychological misunderstanding lies behind the unconscious tendency to treat children with almost the same condescension given to animals, forgetting that children are not a different species of human being, but 'adults' with psychic wholeness in a transforming body.

This same problem extends into the field of psychotherapy where it gives food for thought from another aspect. One result of the influence psychoanalysis has had on medicine is the practice of 'regressing' patients back to childhood to find the cause of conflicts. It is a convenient technique to apply, but a practice to be questioned very seriously by those who see psychotherapy in terms of psychic movement rather than subjective criteria of feeling and functioning better. For out of this regression has grown the singularly unpsychological attitude amongst psychotherapists of blaming the parents for the neuroses or other ailments of their patients. It may gratify certain wishes, but misses the psychotherapeutic needs. And why? Because the problem needing confrontation lies with the psyche of the patient in the present rather than in the behaviour of parents from a distant past. Living earlier as mother and later as maiden expresses the need for many a grown-up 'child' of either sex to reconsider where any blame may lie for neurotic dissatisfactions.

Were the subjects of neurosis in contemporary society really brought up disgracefully by the failure of the woman called mother or the man called father to understand their needs? It would be truer to say that the neurotic attitude is a persistent problem of the individual personality in the present and not an 'error' from the past or, at least, neither more nor less than it might be that of a destined future. The neurotic incapacity of a life seen through the perspective of an inappropriate myth has more to do with the present attitude of the patient than with the 'mistake' of parents in the past. Indeed, if there really was an 'error' in the past, there must already be an 'error' in the future as well, and that in terms of destiny is a very doubtful assumption. In other words, in as far as it concerns psychotherapists, parents do not 'damage their children in the past'. They play their necessary role and thus contribute to making the destiny of patients. This destiny lies irrevocably and for ever in the personality of the neurotic sufferer, even though paradoxically it is in the process of being made in the present.

Time in the context of psychopathology makes its appearance for the most part in disturbances of orientation. The effect is as if a 'moment of eternity' dislocates consciousness and introduces the unfamiliar, disturbing dimension. Periods of 'unreality', states of depersonalisation and the paramnesia of 'déjà vu' phenomena are disorders which reflect the capriciousness of worldly experience when influenced by the madness of the moon. There is an uncanny and at times distressing quality about these symptoms. They are known to accompany various forms of illness, both physical and mental, and, as implied in the myth, must also take some central part in hysteria. But let it not be forgotten that they are not necessarily an indication of pathology. Indeed, with but a small modification, they may become the source of rich reward for the subject. The same uncanny quality that causes distress may under other circumstances transmit unexpected depths of insight and understanding with knowledge beyond that of rational determination. The gift of prophecy and the ability to function on the intuitive level of a medium are also the legacy of Hecate's border.

The nature of Hecate's influence on these mysterious phenomena is described in the myth of Eleusis where, holding a light before the bereaved mother, she confides, 'I heard a voice but did not see with my eyes who it was'. The point is missed if this is assumed to be a literal event of perceiving through the sensations of seeing and hearing, for hearing in this context is a way of psychic communication rather than a function of conscious determination.

Hecate's participation in the crisis has the subtlety of darkness in the way she recognises a presence using the same uncanny perception of the mother who does not need to be awake to perceive her child's distress. The relevant feature of the motif lies in the manner of Hecate's hearing without seeing. This does not mean hearing as a blind person would hear, but rather seeing as a blind, or any other person might 'see' without the use of the familiar sensory channels; perception of the rape in the manner of a medium through darkness rather than light. It marks an entrance into parapsychology and the world of occult phenomena. Who can wonder that Hecate is a patroness of witches?

In spite of the popular idea of the moment that insists on equality, whether of people, sexes or opportunities, there is every indication that not all are blessed to the same degree by each divinity influencing the soul. Hecate is a clear example of this truth in the way some lives more than others fall predominantly under her mediation. Between the darkness of the crescent moon and the invisibility of the underworld lie those fascinating powers that are the preoccupation of spiritualists, clairvoyants, mediums and others belonging to the order of so-called 'psychic' people. Perhaps because of the indefinite, borderline nature of their practices, the word 'psychic' in this context has come to mean spiritual with quasi-theological overtones. Nevertheless, psychic is the adjective in use and psyche, not spirit, is the significant factor. It implies recognition of a 'fourth' dimension for which a prerequisite is the function of extrasensory perception. Clearly not all are equally gifted in this way, but the high percentage found amongst hysteric subjects probably accounts for the reason why hysteria has diagnostically never been far from the borderline.

But what is special about Hecate's distant borders? The threshold qualities of the borderline existence are precarious, especially when these are rendered dark and remote. Hence the ancient custom of dedicating a wayside shrine to Hecate at three-way crossings where the traveller encounters a border and an uncertain choice of ways to proceed. A threshold has been reached, though in fact it is neither here nor there; a 'nowhere' of transition not quite on one side or the other. Those who find themselves in that situation are vulnerable and exposed to unpredictable forces from outside as well as vacillation and instability from within. Fear there may be in plenty, but that is no good reason for the censorship which the borderline has earned as a feature of psychopathology. To some extent the moral judgement arises not from fear so much as the feature of suggestibility, the two-edged potential at its centre. Here lies a well-guarded secret under Hecate's protection, for to grasp the essential psychology of suggestion were almost to reveal the mystery of human nature. From the prejudice it evokes, suggestion would appear to be noticed only for its negative effects and taken for granted under most other circumstances. Psychotherapists tend to regard suggestibility as an unwanted relic of childhood and a weakness to be corrected; 'weak ego' is the term of disapproval applied to those generously imbued with this gift. A different assessment might be forthcoming were it more widely appreciated that suggestibility describes the natural state of artists and other individuals granted a greater than average potential for originality. The same potential lies in hysteria. It does indeed define a specific quality of ego complex, but not necessarily a weakness to be strengthened. If weakness is in some way a troublesome feature, let it be remembered that weakness is not synonymous with suggestibility and the origins must be sought elsewhere.

Suggestion is but one feature of the borderline that contemporary prejudice underestimates or sees functioning in the 'wrong' place. Traditionally this and other gifts of Hecate have been attributed to women, though they are no more the exclusive property of woman than were the ritual practices of Eleusis. But woman, mistakenly assumed to be the sole beneficiary, has frequently been identified in a vague and often derogatory way as intuitive, unpredictable, irrational, illogical, 'deep', mediumistic. These qualities are assumed incorrectly to hinder rational, intellectual functioning. Hysteria may from its early beginnings have been associated exclusively with woman, but the great mistake has always been to underestimate the gifts it offers.

Exceptions abound and never more plentifully than when prejudice has voiced the rule. The borderline qualities are threatening, but they are also fascinating when they appear as the gift of an 'extra' sense. The medium and the clairvoyant, well blessed with the extra sense, have for a long time practised their arts in the shadow, assumed to be of little importance and of intellectual inferiority; but in the present time they begin to thrive on a new-found popularity, of which some, but not all, can be attributed to hysteric over-enthusiasm.

There is no direct mention of Hecate's name in the hysteric myth although there is ample evidence of that presence in the psycho-pathology, as if her name had been taken in vain. One of the more immediate expressions of this presence is in the disorders that go by the medical name of 'altered states of consciousness'. Sympto-matically this covers a wide area of psychopathology including that of hysteria, where altered consciousness is always assumed to play a subsidiary role to sex and suffocation. This is an unsound assump-tion, although an unprejudiced look will show that it is equally prominent in all the changing phases of that disease. The quality of the altered consciousness demonstrates hysteria's own particular form of madness that could well be called lunacy in the best meaning of that word. Some comment on its nature appears in the following dream of a woman prone to somnambulism in the form of hysteric trances at inopportune moments:

'I was a young girl picking flowers in a meadow. As I approached to pick a flower it receded; it rose into the sky where it became the moon.'

Certain features of this image are unmistakable in their likeness to the myth of Persephone at play, even though there is a fundamental difference in that here they belong to the dream of a patient and not to a divine myth. Particularly striking is the fact that, where dream and myth differ, the features of the dream resemble more the human myth of hysteria than that of Eleusis. The young girl is alone in a meadow and the earth does not open in rape. She is not dragged downwards and the flower of her choice levitates. Something belong-ing on earth is displaced into the sky and, in terms of the myth of Eleusis something destined for movement into the underworld remains unmoved on earth. It is as if a divine myth had been distorted and an ordinary event had become extraordinary and fantastic.

The pattern of events in the dream is like Hecate's participation in an hysteric illusion. Instead of being companion to the flower-like maiden, she as it were 'rapes' it to herself. In much the same way a flower floating upwards is a trick of the moon reflecting to some extent the fantastic and illusionary quality of consciousness in fugues, 'absences', somnambulism, multiple personalities and trances, all of which, together with the spell-casting of witches, have found their way into hysteria. But the hazard of suggestion must be reckoned with in this image. Hysteria is a mimic and needs the constant reminder that it is not the same as that which it mimics. An altered consciousness is not in itself an expression of hysteria. On the contrary, it is a state common to many pathologies bearing the seal of the threefold goddess. There is none the less a kinship between hysteria and twilight states of consciousness. This dream brings light to bear on the subject through its kinship to the myth.

Hecate, says Homer, 'with much affection for the daughter of sacred Demeter . . . precedes and follows'. In other words, the myth, in describing the divine companionship, brings emphasis to the mystery of time and space. How is it possible to precede and follow at the same time? Facing both ways from a position in the middle is a metaphoric representation of the predicament in which we live, with the present that extends into memories of the past and anticipations of the future. Hecate defines the borders of those areas; she is the *temenos*, as it were, that allows an eternal present to be in serial time. Without this essential co-operation of Hecate in the image, the hysteric perspective sets a scene with uncertain borders giving an unseemly, even ostentatious, appearance to the positioning and timing of events. An ordinary experience is charged with the mystery of occult powers and becomes sensational, but at the same time lacks serious significance; disembodied spirits haunt with thrilling effect, but little conviction; synchronicity abounds when a profusion of coincidences take on special, but unwarranted, importance. A theatrical exaggeration with a corresponding poverty of sincerity is the manner of communication. The effects are exciting and the impression of time is unruly: fascinating, but not convincing.

Another way to describe the perspective of hysteric distortion would be to say that events are near to the realm of witchery, yet not quite of it. Under these circumstances the magic infecting the phenomena does not lie in the service of evil as such, but in hysteric simulation. It is important to grasp this distinction. Hysteria gives an impression which, often assessed through prejudice, is assumed to be deliberately malign or destructive when in truth it is rather an inappropriate nuisance. In the same way that not every emotional outburst is hysteric, so the characteristics here are on no account to be confused with the wiles of real witchery any more than with the communications of a medium or the pronouncements of an oracle. Magic divinatory practices may co-exist with various forms of sickness or health, but are not necessarily hysteric.

In view of the alliance between Hecate and the witch, it was almost inevitable that hysteria would at some time participate in a sinister form of magic. This it did effectively in the course of mediaeval history by becoming one with the witch. The hysteric burning of witches was an injustice of unparalleled cruelty and at the same time a monument to a madness that spread like an infectious epidemic. Hysteria was known as a disorder of women and witches were women infidels who had entered a lustful pact with the Devil. What could be more natural than that a misrepresentation through the obscurity of the mythic background should portray the two as synonymous? In this way hysteric disease came indirectly to be identified with a sin of heresy and burning at the stake was the current 'treatment'. According to descriptions from that time, the regular signs and symptoms of hysteria were clearly defined, but with the addition of a new feature: it was regarded as pathognomonic of the disease if areas of the skin surface proved anaesthetic to pinpricks. Not so clear in this situation, but never called into doubt, was the question of where the diagnosis should really have been applied. Women were infected with hysteria through the evil spells of another woman who was a witch; but it is unclear from the accounts which of the two, patient or witch, was the subject of the disease. Both bore the diagnostic stigmata and some of the victims were ready to boast that they were in sexual alliance with the Devil after the manner of witches. On this evidence the hysteria must have been common to both parties, and it sounds infectious. But the question is, how far did the infection extend and where exactly was the hysteria? Those in authority began to see it everywhere except in themselves, though their own behaviour was such that they were not above suspicion. For the most part the authority consisted of men, and men were anyway granted immunity from hysteria and so from examination. It is interesting to speculate how the accusers would have fared had they, too, submitted to the same investigations as the women who were their victims, for hysteria was 'in the air' as well as in the patients.

Reading the literature on psychopathology it is easy to jump to the conclusion that the Inquisition was responsible for the burning of women convicted of hysteria and so of witchery. Certainly over the major part of Europe, including those countries where the impact of the Inquisition was most immediate, the connection between the two was so indirect and remote that any such accusation is unwarranted. Ecclesiastic authority was indeed responsible for widespread suffering and its Inquisition executed many heretics by burning, but the jurisdiction over hysteria was negligible. In these matters the temporal laws of the land were responsible for the executions even though the sentences carried the stigma of co-operating wilfully with the Devil. Only in so far as heresy was a crime against the State might there be some indirect justification for involving the Inquisition in blame. But, wherever the blame may fall, those women inflicted with hysteria were burned none the less and the appalling miscarriage of justice carries the responsibility of a grave error in the name of spiritual betterment.

One feature of particular interest from accounts of the period is the impression of a psychic epidemic having broken out. As the infection in this case was hysteria, it might understandably be regarded as a mass hysteria. But is that really the meaning of mass hysteria? There is room for doubt. The diagnosis proves to be fraught with as much difficulty in the mass as in the individual. For example, is hysteria the explanation for the emotional reactions of a football crowd, for the conversions of an evangelist revival meeting and for an epidemic of fainting in a school? The answer is not immediately obvious.

It seems a pity to leave the question as it stands, for the unsatisfactory conclusion may be drawn that there is no difference between mass hysteria and any other phenomena of mass psychology. The diagnosis may unfortunately rest on a personal prejudice: if we don't like football, then the crowds are hysteric; if we don't like hysteria in certain places, then the school epidemic is conveniently caused by a virus.

Mass psychology always contains a high degree of suggestibility and depends on a darkened, yet receptive, quality of consciousness for its effects. Mass hysteria, on the other hand, must mean a mass of people infected with hysteria. How then do the two differ? They share certain features of consciousness in common though, as already noted, suggestibility and a somnambulistic consciousness are not the sole prerogative of hysteria. Certainly hysteria is not the factor common to the three different crowds. Furthermore, not all mass psychology is hysteria though, as with the individual, it may exist with hysteria. To differentiate the two is an uncommonly difficult and delicate task. In the occasional school epidemic, for example, the atmosphere of hysteria is heavy with the way the sufferers mimic their neighbours rather than a disease. That impression is not quite so convincing in the revivalist meeting, whereas in the case of the football crowd it is not prominent, yet cannot be altogether excluded.

One diagnostic pitfall making a clear outcome very difficult to achieve follows from the medical attitude towards differential diagnosis which sees its responsibility to decide which of two (or more) diseases is manifest. In the case of hysteria, both in the mass and the individual, the question is not, 'is that hysteria or something else?' but, 'is hysteria present or not?' Witch hunting was no exception. In that tragedy of sickening proportions the intentions of the temporal lawmakers cannot have been only the outcome of hysteria. It is nevertheless unthinkable that a phenomenon on such a massive scale and centred around hysteria should not in some measure be infected with that hysteria. From a diagnostic point of view, it is sometimes an unconscious hysteric mimicry and sometimes a more genuine involvement. But the important point is to avoid the error of a careless assumption that all mass psychology is mass hysteria.

Witch hunting waxed slowly to a climax and subsided. Soon it was of little interest and disappeared, like other epidemics, almost as if nothing had happened. But certain matters of Church and State were more clearly defined when hysteria returned once more into the hands of the medical profession. A chapter in the mythology of the disease came to a close and hysteria was free for other ventures in other fields, leaving once again the feeling that it is more than an illness in the accepted sense of the word.

7

RESPECTABLE SORCERY

The transformations that took place in hysteria from mediaeval to modern times must to some extent have reflected those taking place in the whole field of medicine during that great period of change. The era, leading into the time of the Enlightenment, was one of intense scientific interest; an historic period of singular importance in which hysteria found its setting just as surely as in the times of witch hunting. Scientific advancement is the rational explanation for the changing times, but a more discerning age sees beneath the surface of the external events the archetypal patterns playing their parts in an evolving cultural scene and influencing appearances in a way that even science could not control. Never has hysteria found more precise definition as a distinct entity of disease or been more enthusiastically accepted than during this period. It was regarded as a real illness in the same way as any other in the classification of disease. Yet in spite of clinical precision, the nature of hysteria continued to raise difficulties and to cast doubts on its authenticity in the field of pathology.

With regard to the archetypal patterning of hysteria, the image of Hecate continued to exert its influence in a prominent way long after the time of witch hunting. Hecate's role is less noticeable (though always present) in the earlier and ancient history of the disease than in later centuries, when altered states of consciousness became a feature of increasing importance beside the more familiar physical symptoms of hysteria. To some extent the same may be said of many other diseases, for the nature of consciousness was gaining interest and importance at this time, largely as a result of psychology beginning to gain recognition in the field of medicine. This brought no new diagnostic additions for hysteria, but rather a change in emphasis within the existing pattern of symptoms and signs.

Alteration of consciousness was a feature of hysteria even at the time of its early records. The seizure and the epileptiform fits described by physicians of the Hippocratic era bear testimony to this, while the researches of Galen confirmed different levels of consciousness in hysteria as diagnostic of different clinical categories. These characteristics were taken for granted until the end of the eighteenth century when a more psychological appreciation of conscious states brought greater differentiation. It was responsible for an altogether more refined classification of diseases in general; a scientific revisioning of that field in which hysteria played a surprisingly large and to a great extent un-recognised part.

Three significant events coincided in that period of history to establish that hysteria was to the forefront: the last burning of a witch in Europe, the appearance of the term 'neurosis' in the medical vocabulary and an official acceptance of the name 'hysteria' rather than 'hysteric suffocation' to define that specific item of disease. The events in themselves were not outstanding, but in retrospect their coincidence for the meaning of hysteria is noteworthy. The witch hunt ended and a new venture with a more scientifically acceptable form of magic began.

The following dream sheds light on the nature of consciousness which, at this time of transition, was a prominent feature of hysteria. As the dream itself says, it is essentially about hysteria; it provides a guiding thread through a dimly lit labyrinth and touches on the theme of changing consciousness as seen from its mythic background. This dream says much about the nature of hysterià in general as well as aiding the understanding for this particular period of its history of hysteria's relations with other illnesses.

'In an interview with the doctor, I said, "I want to tell you about my hysteria". I felt the mad laughter coming over me and became frightened I would not be able to speak for laughing. I felt hysterical. At that moment the sky changed; it went black, the stars came out, the room was changed into what appeared to be an astronomer's observation post. There was no need for telescopes, for the stars seemed nearer and easier to observe. I could not speak for a moment, the vision was so awe-inspiring and beautiful. It became so overpowering that I gasped and fainted away.'

The dream is not making a diagnosis, but wants to tell about hysteria. In the event nothing is said, for hysteria puts an abrupt end to this standard manner of communication. The circumstances are described in terms of light. Daylight clarity vanishes and the hysteria appears as a confrontation with the night sky where a relative darkness prevails. To put this in another way, the hysteria is an encounter with the stars, an experience with the light of darkness rather than the light of day. The impact of the transition from one state to the other is sudden, sensational and overwhelming. Indeed, though not stated as such in the dream, it is even violent and possessive, like a rape; not, of course, the typical violation perpetrated by a male deity, but a 'rape' by the darkness of the night ruled over by the mother goddess, Hecate. It brings to mind the myth of hysteria in which a maiden is 'raped', as it were, by a mother rather than male intruder.

This dream depicts a remarkable phenomenon. The encounter with the stars is itself an unusual and surprising experience. It establishes that the stars, the light of darkness, set the hysteric scene. The dream also tells of a transformation from a consulting room into what appears to be an astronomer's observation post where everything is nearer and easier to see. One of the surprising experiences is that of the viewpoint being an observatory, for from here a closer and easier view of the sky may be expected with the conventional use of a telescope. But telescopes, it says, are not necessary. Vision, in other words, is with the natural equipment of the astrologer rather than the artificial enlarging apparatus of the astronomer. The effects of this transformation are deceptive. At first glance the stars seem to be bigger and more immediate, but on closer inspection that proves not to be the case. A different perspective has altered perception and the result is an hysteric illness in which the stars are in fact no more immediate than when viewed from an observatory.

With the changing features of the consulting room, this dream confirms a characteristic feature long attributed to subjects of hysteria. The imagery defines the subtle deception that appears when hysteria introduces exaggeration and a distorted sense of location. Situations seem to be a bit larger than life and at the same time there is an illusion of closeness. It brings to mind the picture described in medical textbooks as the contrast between an actual shallowness of feelings and the intensity with which they are demonstrated. The dream is also confirmation that with regard to time and space, things are not quite as they seem to be in hysteria.

Astrology was already an established science by the time of hysteria's early records. Originally the stars it studied were experienced as having a more immediate and compulsive influence on human life than the majority of astrologers would now claim. The compulsion is in fact the same today as it was in ancient times, but the astrological appreciation of its effects has changed considerably. The astral influence on the personality, though still of central importance, is no longer considered by many to be as direct as it was in those ancient times. Probably the invention of the telescope was instrumental in robbing them astrologically of some former glory. Scientific objectivity brought fresh imagination to space and hastened the slow process of interpolating psyche between the stars and their victims.

A factor of even greater significance than the telescope in robbing the stars of their immediate effect was the work of alchemy in mediaeval times. It marked the beginning of a process which was later to introduce psychology into the study of astrology. In the earnest endeavours of those devout alchemists to attain the *lapis philosophorum*, the stars appeared to them as scintillae or sparks in the arcane substance of the opus, and with this vision came insight.

The works and writings of the famous physician Paracelsus tell how he was able to move the image a step beyond the scintillae by recognising the stars in the setting of an 'inner firmament'. Astral influence was no longer limited to magic coming directly from the heavens, but was joined by that of an inner firmament within the human soul, a microcosm resembling the outer heavens in all its aspects. The astute observations of Paracelsus made him a more prominent figure than his colleagues as a forerunner of the psychological work to come.

This brief digression into astrology and alchemy is not an idle, loose association, for it is immediately relevant to the image of the dream. The dark psyche, as in the dreamer's vision, is a night sky strewn with stars. It is, in other words, an archetypal image with dots of light in an overwhelming darkness expressing the nature of isolated, dissociated phenomena of consciousness within that psyche; an archetypal image of how archetypes appear. This, the dream says, is in some way directly relevant to hysteria.

Formulations change and understanding grows in sophistication, but one feature of the stars has remained the same for the astrologer, the alchemist and the modern psychologist: each in his own way maintains a high degree of respect for the power of astral compulsion. The astrologer sees in this a dependence of character and of destiny on certain moments of time in relation to the stars. The same compulsive force for the psychologist lies in the archetypal basis of personality manifesting beyond the powers of the human will and often in symptoms of neurosis or other psychopathologies. But, regardless of how this situation may be understood, the ancient religions of the world have always sought to free humanity from the compulsion of the stars. Those endeavours in the form of modern psychotherapy continue into the present day to rescue victims from blind, overwhelming compulsions and to promote stability in the face of emotional imbalance.

Following on from this image of 'astral' influence as understood by physicians ancient and modern, astrologers, alchemists and psychologists, it can be no surprise that psychiatric descriptions of hysteria in recent times have stressed a state of limited self-control with an archaic quality of consciousness under the dominance of affects and fantasies. It has earned this reputation because hysteria shares with certain other psychopathologies the same qualities of consciousness as those portrayed in the foregoing dream. Those under the compulsion of the stars not only experience an altered state of consciousness, but reduction of self-control as they become victims of the archetypal world of the psyche and the demands of collective conscious expectations.

It would be unthinkable to discuss any matter of medicine from the eighteenth century without reference to magnetism. As the last of the witches was burned, there arose from the ashes, as it were, the image of Anton Mesmer (1734–1815), the German physician whose discovery of animal magnetism in the field of therapeutics proves to be an unforgettable milestone in the history of medicine in spite of the strong disapproval it met from the medical profession. The antagonistic reactions of the scientific world were such that contemporary and future generations of physicians were unable to take this form of therapy seriously, let alone to accept it within the field of medicine. Mesmer's magnetism won small appreciation, but its appearance on the scene proved nevertheless to be a great historic innovation and a great moment for hysteria. The affinity between the two is not hard to find when seen from the perspective of Hecate.

From its beginning, the fascination of magic and mystery surrounded Mesmer's work. Animal magnetism caught the public fancy, as it still does today, with its sensational practices belonging to the shadier side – now called less dubiously the 'fringe' side – of medicine. Originally it was used as an alternative method of treatment to that of driving out, or exorcising, evil spirits. Exorcism was the accepted practice in certain disorders which, as a result of Mesmer's treatment, were recognised thereafter as mental disturbances rather than inflictions of divine intervention. In this way magnetism was instrumental in expanding the field of medicine to include illnesses previously considered to be outside its jurisdiction. It may at the same time claim to be the successor to the magic of the witch. Magnetism as it looks today is one of the innumerable different methods of psychotherapy related distantly to hypnosis and associated vaguely with the doubtful dealings of the charlatan. The practices – then as now – touch on the psychology of trance, but in a way that carries faintly occult, rather than scientific, overtones.

From the point of view of hysteria, the arrival of animal magnetism coincided with the official recognition of that disease appearing in man as well as woman. It was perhaps as a result of overcoming this sexual prejudice that the understanding of hysteria changed with the aid of magnetism from condemnation of the witch's magic to recognition as a sort of respectable sorcery in the form of hypnotism.

The fate of hysteria is closely linked with the discovery of the disease entity, neurosis, and the unorthodox therapy, animal magnetism. Some further consideration of these two new arrivals in more detail is necessary here the better to understand the role of hysteria. It introduces the term somnambulism, the generic name for the altered states of consciousness that include not only the dream quoted that tells of hysteria, but also neurosis and magnetism. The theme of somnambulism came much to the forefront for discussion and research in medical practice during the eighteenth and nineteenth centuries. A wide range of disorders is included under the term, all of which have at one time or another found association, if not identification, with hysteria. This has been the source of much diagnostic discomfort and interest centred around the difficulty presented by hysteric deception. Neurosis and magnetism – later to be joined by hypnosis – represent that quality of consciousness that is the soil in which the fateful attachments to hysteria grew. The course of their history is difficult to follow, but ultimately it proves to be a rewarding study in the nature of hysteria.

Although with the passage of time hysteria was exonerated from charges of witchery, the magic quality of its dealings in matters of illness began to follow a variation on the theme of sorcery. The event which proved to bear much relevance for the fate of hysteria was the discovery, within the field of neurology, of neurosis as a new category of illness. This discovery meant the acknowledgement of many functional symptoms not previously accepted as authentic medical pathology. To accept this uncharacteristic ailment was in many ways a momentous step for scientific medicine. Uncertainty as to its nature was never far away and it is not surprising that neurosis, like hysteria, proved ultimately to be suspect as a true entity of disease.

First use of the word 'neurosis' has been attributed to the Scottish physician William Cullen (1710–90), who ascribed to it certain disorders of the nervous system appearing without evidence of organic cause. Whether or not it was known to him at the time, his discovery and its acceptance coincided with Mesmer's not-so-readily accepted discovery of animal magnetism. Much credit is due to the innovators of these two contributions to medicine. Cullen, giving a new formulation to psychic influence in disease, and Mesmer, introducing a scientifically orientated method of treatment for conditions many of which were considered previously to be outside the province of medicine, opened a new perspective on psychological medicine and established the discoveries as forerunners of modern psychotherapy.

A new scene opened up for hysteria. Neurosis and animal magnetism were indeed an irresistible draw, for between them they were never far from showing that quality of magic which runs throughout the story of healing. In the case of Mesmer's magnet, this found expression as the 'crisis', the altered consciousness, sometimes accompanied by convulsions, in patients in a state of trance or mesmerised sleep. But that dramatic picture was not new to medicine. Similar 'crises' were familiar from previous centuries, not only in certain forms of hysteria, but in the altered state of consciousness known to accompany magic treatments by shamans and witch doctors as well as in the more orthodox ways of exorcism. The element of magic, though freely acknowledged in the primitive tribal healing, avoided open recognition of its presence in the more sophisticated procedure of mesmerism and in all subsequent developments of this practice.

By the beginning of the nineteenth century, researches had moved Mesmer's magic a step forwards and established that a similar state of trance could be induced by other techniques and even without the use of magnets. Much credit for this work must go to Mesmer's ardent admirer, the Marquis de Puyséqur (1755–1848), who was one amongst several other workers in this field in France and Germany. Puyséqur gained a wide following, though his methods, like those of his mentor, were for the most part not accepted in medical circles. They were nevertheless instrumental in inspiring a new interest in the working of the mind. The induced trance was a form of somnambulism similar to many other states of altered consciousness found in 'twilight' experiences, fugues and phenomena of multiple personality. This field became the material for researches into the psychology of medicine and was indeed for many decades the only way open to investigation of the unconscious psyche. Somnambulism was the 'royal road' at that time, as later the dream became for Freud and the complex for Jung. But, of all the states included under this heading, the most significant for the future of hysteria was the trance of animal magnetism. The discovery of this particular artificially induced form of somnambulism was the immediate forerunner of the state that the English physician James Braid (1795–1860), in 1843, called 'hypnosis'. In this way Braid paved the most direct path for sorcery to become acceptable in scientific circles.

Hysteria had always been a disorder of unreliable content and, as ever more areas of pathology were differentiated into a refined classification of diagnoses, this unreliability grew more prominent. It seemed moderately clear that hysteria was an authentic disease, but at the same time it seemed that hysteria was quietly and furtively becoming many different things. Though not quite definable, but none the less real, there was always a lingering doubt to prompt the question, what really is this disease? The picture in retrospect shows how deception lies in the strange association hysteria formed with somnambulism, itself an ill-defined area of pathology.

Magnetism and neurosis marked two distinct paths of development in medicine taking place simultaneously. That followed by neurosis was closer to orthodox medical teaching. It proved to be an aid to differentiation of psychogenic illness by a process of sifting and exclusion as, slowly, organic causes were discovered for many syndromes previously thought to have been neuroses.

Advancements in endocrinology and refined investigations into neurology accounted for many; but the matter of special interest and importance for the study of hysteria was the recognition by the German psychiatrist, Emil Kraepelin (1856–1926), of the so-called endogenous illnesses, dementia praecox and manic-depressive psychosis. These pathologies, though still clearly understandable under the term 'functional illness', were now placed amongst the psychoses and considered to be of a different nature to neurosis.

One reason why the diagnostic differentiation of the endogenous psychoses within the field of neurosis has never been as easy an undertaking as it might seem, is that the obscuring influence of hysteria is never far away. Its close affinity with neurosis meant that hysteria would inevitably be drawn towards severe mental disturbances. This fact was well recognised in psychiatric circles, but little appreciated amongst members of the non-medical public, who have always regarded hysteria as mild and not quite real. Yet hysteria could indeed reach threatening proportions and, until the middle of the twentieth century, held an important place in the differential diagnosis of insanity. The characteristics of its role are exemplified by the high emotionality and tension always surrounding the theme of suicide. Those difficult cases, when not considered to be in immediate danger from psychotic depression, were explained away as hysteria and the threat of suicide as a demand for attention rather than an earnest intent. The difficulty has always been to know where the psychosis begins and the hysteria ends. Does one state really become the other?

That association with severe mental disturbances close to, and seeming sometimes to become, psychosis, produced the doubtful diagnosis of 'borderline' case. For a time hysteria itself was the borderline state, but the assumption that it could readily step over the border into psychosis made for a distorted impression of closeness between the two. The idea that one might turn into the other was an oversimplification and missed the important fact that the two different states might co-exist. Hysteria is no longer recognised as an official diagnosis, but the 'borderline' continues to exist for the advantage of those unable or reluctant to make a diagnostic decision. In some circles it has also become the definition of a personality disorder of considerable severity. It is not difficult to sense the obscurity of Hecate's borderline activities in the vicinity.

Hysteria's relations with neurosis were of longer duration, more intimate and more entangled than with psychosis. They reached a pinnacle in the work of Freud, who chose hysteria as the foundation on which to build psychoanalysis. With the growth of psychoanalysis, there evolved the most comprehensive theory of neurosis ever to exist. If hysteria's identification with neurosis had not occurred previously to this work, Freud would surely have brought about that union.

The image of neurosis changed dramatically from its birth as an organic disease of the nervous system to one belonging to the more spiritual realms of psychologically orientated illness. It was during this slow change that hysteria moved from a close association to virtually an identity with neurosis; indeed, to the extent that it is recognised at all, hysteria is still assumed to be a neurosis.

The alliance with magnetism followed a different path. Magnetism wandered at first through areas of practice unacceptable to medicine and later gained recognition as hypnosis. As might be expected from the unpredictable twilight quality of consciousness in hypnosis, the effects, though sensational, made at first little serious impact on the scientific world of medicine. It was largely thanks to the researches of Charcot, an enthusiastic promoter of its cause, that hypnosis eventually found medical acceptance. Charcot's neurological interest led first to the study of hysteria and then to hypnosis. He reached the conclusion that true hypnosis could be induced only in hysteric subjects; that there was, in other words, a close kinship of partial identity between the two. It meant that in a short space of time towards the end of the nineteenth century, hysteria had successfully identified itself with both neurosis and hypnosis. The two paths of development started by Cullen and Mesmer came together in hysteria, albeit for a short period.

The psychological term that leaps to mind in any discussion on somnambulism is *abaissement du niveau mental*. Jung found this lowered level of consciousness to be a ready form of description in certain psychopathologies, especially psychoses and neuroses, and made frequent reference throughout his writings to *abaissement*, each time with a respectful recognition of Pierre Janet (1859–1947), the originator of the term. By *abaissement* Janet meant a depression, a lowering of consciousness with a reduction of attention. *Abaissement*, he said, is a constant characteristic of neurosis; not, as often assumed, simply a cause, but one of what Janet called the regular stigmata of neurosis. If this observation is heard in association with the qualities of consciousness portrayed earlier in the dream of hysteria, it is small wonder that hysteria shared such close kinship with neurosis.

With hypnosis the attraction is even more pronounced, for there are two particular features that hypnosis shares in common with hysteria to a greater degree than with other states of somnambulism. They are an openness to suggestion and a readiness to theatrical effect. Indeed it is a likely matter of speculation that hysteria was influential in extending hypnosis from the consulting room to the theatre stage, where it continues to exercise the irresistible fascination of magic.

Hypnosis is well equipped for the stage. It has a theatrical way of showing time not simply as a past, present and future, but as a mixture of all three at once, while the qualities of space are correspondingly irregular. Vision in hypnosis is apparently capable of going through solid objects or round corners, even of confirming something to be in two places at the same time. The uncanny effects it produces are not unlike certain features already attributed to hysteria. They, too, bear striking resemblance to the image of Hecate. Both hysteria and hypnosis may claim witch-like dealings conducted from the crescent of the dark moon, where consciousness is correspondingly dark and constrained to reflect what it receives: a model of suggestibility.

The kinship is striking and archetypally convincing. The qualities of hysteric consciousness are similar to those of hypnosis in their relations to time and space and in their mysterious communication with the spirits of the environment. Hysteria, like hypnosis, has its stage and its audience. It also shares with certain other phenomena of somnambulism the psychic connection with Hecate's 'nightly swarm of ghosts' that mediates perceptions outside the awareness of others, as in the hysteric ability to pick up shadowy meanings through closed doors or the awareness of a presence in an empty room. A closely related phenomenon, holding great potential for a psychotherapist confronting hysteria, is the capacity for provoking antagonism by reacting instinctively to hidden, undesirable shadow qualities in those whom they meet. These roles may be reversed if in the psychotherapy the hysteria in the personality is stronger on the side of the patient, whose uncanny insight and ability touches – albeit to a large extent unconsciously – on the physician's inferiority, much to the discomfort of the latter.

The likenesses that exist between hysteria and hypnosis are concerned essentially with states of consciousness rather than physical symptoms. Lying outside the familiar ground of hysteric mimicry, they demonstrate other aspects of the unpredictable and transitory nature of hysteria. The closer the study, the more hysteria seems to oscillate in a disconcerting way between being everywhere and nowhere, as if it were the mercurial psyche itself. But hysteria is not that elusive, mysterious substance we call the psyche, which, like quicksilver, cannot be grasped. Hysteria can be seen and grasped, but it has the gift of sudden disappearance, like a water nymph or nature spirit, leaving no trace and no certainty of return. There is a glimpse of this characteristic in the dream of hysteria quoted earlier wherein the change of perspective is followed by disappearance in oblivion. This is not a characteristic of hypnosis. With hysteria, on the other hand, it appears not only subjectively in those afflicted, but in the disease itself as confronted by the physician or others. Subjects of hysteria know the undesirable experience of suddenly 'not being there'. Their hysteric, though gifted, insights and understandings are restricted by a sense of incapacitation and the subjective impression of not quite existing. Disorientation, trance-like states and even loss of consciousness are often a part of the picture. Hysteria may bring wonderful gifts, but the price is an unwelcome lack of stability in consciousness with which to use them. Objectively, those who confront hysteria for investigation or treatment know how they may lose sight of their diagnosis as they realise suddenly that they are deluded. The presenting features of the patient are in fact those of healthy human characteristics not indicative of any pathology. The hysteria has disappeared abruptly down a hole. Why, after all, should highly emotional behaviour in a suggestible subject be hysteria? Why indeed; but then, with equal abruptness, hysteria reappears as the appropriate diagnosis. Yes or no? The changing impression is as disconcerting for the onlooker as for the patient. Like the liquid flame of a log fire, this disease vanishes before the eyes, only to reappear as it was before.

The 'water-nymph' characteristic of hysteria has followed the path of medicine through many changing scenes while frustrating its practitioners on the way. Many syndromes of illness have at different times been attributed to hysteria only to reveal themselves later as belonging to other pathologies. This sounds like a form of treachery: a dishonest diversion with intent to mislead. Yet such immoral behaviour does not belong to hysteria. It has an archetypal role to play that transcends the wilful decisions and designs of those it involves. Were it not for the continuity of hysteria, rather than its apparent inconsistency, it is probable that the history of magnetism and neurosis would read today only as a series of unrelated events in which many significant details would forfeit their relevance. But the fact is that hysteria appeared first in one and then in the other and, after a mysterious participation, withdrew or, more accurately, was dismissed by each of them in turn. When eventually hysteria parted company with Freud's psychoneurosis and various syndromes of neurology, the field of neurotic disorders of necessity underwent revision and took on a different meaning that led to refinements in the psychological understanding of personality. Hysteria itself remained, like a catalyst, untouched in the process, while the erstwhile hosts continued with a new-found authority. For hysteria is neither hypnosis nor neurosis, neither somnambulism nor conversion symptoms. It is, on the other hand, a quality of character that may assert itself and add hysteria to each pathology.

In the realm of illness, hysteria's participation with catalytic detachment goes far towards explaining its Proteus-like existence over many centuries. Much has been made of the shortcomings in diagnostic techniques and of the different outcome if these past experiences of hysteria could have had the benefit of contemporary scientific precision; but such speculation misses the historic significance and the relevance of hysteria's role. Of crucial importance is the realisation that the changing forms of the disease have in general never implied a wrong diagnosis, as many people are ready to assume. Hysteria was indeed each of the syndromes it was said to be at different periods – a displaced womb, a convulsive seizure, a witch's spell, hypochondria, hypnosis or neurosis – by means of its ability to feign identity. It was also *not* these syndromes, as later events established after the disappearance of hysteria. Following hysteria's withdrawal, the status quo of the pathologies remained unchanged but left with a better appreciation of their reality; more precisely, nothing changed the syndromes and that paradoxical 'nothing' is hysteria.

In spite of generations of doubts cast on the authenticity of hysteria, only in the twentieth century did it receive any official medical rejection. The strongest influence on the decision grew not, as might be assumed, from its deceptive powers of identification, but its readiness to suggestion. The end was already in sight when physicians realised that suggestion was not a pathological condition peculiar to hysteria and hypnosis, but a natural characteristic of all human beings. It paved the way for the first authoritative declaration that hysteria was in fact not a disease as such, but a particular quality of personality, meaning that everyone is potentially hysteric, though some more than others. In the light of events to come, this understanding of suggestion was the most effective doubt cast on hysteria's authenticity. Little more than half a century later it ceased to be recognised officially in many circles of medicine as an individual illness. It would, however, be careless to assume that hysteria no longer exists. The only clear communication on the subject is that a time came when the majority of the medical profession were agreed no longer to accept this wayward child as a illness in its own right.

Even though it has always been a suspect disease, any decision not to recognise hysteria still comes as a surprise. The word rings with the familiarity of many centuries and has established its own authority. The form in which it was recognised was always a very variable factor in its existence, likening it to the ways of Proteus. According to dictionaries, the word 'hysteria' as the definition of a specific disease entered general usage only at the end of the eighteenth century. Originally, the wandering womb was a pathology of hysteric suffocation rather than a disease called 'hysteria', though in all probability the term 'hysteria' was, then as now, in use to describe the circumstances, whatever they may have been, when the hysteric characteristics were manifested in the mass or individual. History is unclear in that respect; but the nature of the myth is also unclear and in many respects unconvincing. No-one can be surprised that hysteria as an individual entity of illness had to go, for in truth it was never really there.

The present state of definition seems to imply that the role of hysteria in medicine is all but finished. Can this be true? To judge from the origins and history of hysteria, there is still every probability that it will appear again and command attention in one guise or another. As Pierre Janet observed, 'The word "hysteria" should be preserved, although its primitive meaning has much changed. It would be difficult to modify it nowadays, and truly it has so great and beautiful a history that it would be painful to give it up' (Janet 1901, p. 517). How appropriate that observation remains in the present day! It would not only be painful, but downright incorrect to give it up, for hysteria exists and its role, even in medicine, is not yet finished.

It is also not finished with regard to discussion on its myth. If at best hysteria is but an imitation of disease, there remains the important question of whether this differs in any way from the medical state of malingering.

8

A HOLE IN ONE

There is at the present time a cultural trend in many parts of the world that gives an exaggerated, almost hysterical, value to the pursuit of games. Golf is prominent on that scene. The popularity of this game, though meteoric in its rise, must still leave many people so far distant from such interests that they are unaware of the pun in the title of this essay. A hole in *one* suggests that there is no hole in the *other*; but it is also a term, familiar to golfers the world over, meaning that one shot has sufficed to guide the ball into the hole when, under more ordinary circumstances, at least three would normally be required. It implies a very advantageous way of reaching the goal. Both meanings within the title are appropriate in this setting and are relevant to a goal in the study of hysteria.

To dwell on the contrast between the myths of hysteria and Eleusis is to awaken a hint of hidden fraudulence. The image that they present together is such that it conjures an impression of one myth trying to pose as the other. As detail is more comprehensive in that of Eleusis, it is inevitable that any suspicion of misrepresentation falls on hysteria. Whether or not that suspicion is justified remains to be seen, but certainly, when contrasted with the myth of Eleusis, there is an illusion of deficiency in the myth of hysteria; an impression that it is incomplete beside the other. The illusion goes far towards making intelligible why it is that hysteria is never wanting in explanations, yet apparently ever reluctant to reveal its nature.

In many ways negation is a better word to describe the myth of hysteria than deficiency, for it implies an absence with a sense of nothingness. The advantage in this context that it possesses over deficiency lies in that reference to nothingness, not simply implying no existence, but rather a presence implied by outline. A hole in the wall is far from easy to define. An attempt coming close to it (in terms rather more imposing than that which deficiency warrants) is that of a partial negation in the totality of the surrounding positive circumstances. The negation conveys the nothingness, but the hole is there just the same; we can bear witness to its existence. The same may be said of hysteria, which, like the hole, is strangely difficult to define though, judging by the frequent use of the word, apparently easy to recognise.

The particular importance of negation for hysteria reveals itself when the myths are placed together – one on top of the other, as it were. It emphasises the illusion of deficiency; of one being a replica of the other with a hole in it. If this bears any significance for hysteria, it will surely be found by directing attention not towards the hole itself, but towards the surrounding, positive circumstances. For hysteria, when once recognised, has a characteristic way of dis-appearing suddenly into that nothingness of the hole. The outline brings the nature of hysteria into relief and provides a thread of continuity to hold when the hysteria has, unpredictably, vanished from view.

With regard to psychopathology, a peculiar and, to say the least, unfamiliar image begins to emerge. Can it be that a myth has a hole in it? Is not the myth of hysteria complete within itself? Of more immediate importance than a direct answer to either of those questions is the further study in contrast; for the myth of Eleusis gives form and substance to all that seems to be negated. Standing out from the place of negation is a silhouette in the form of Hades and the Rape. Though its meaning may not be instantly apparent, this silhouette bears direct reference to the body; reference in terms not only of the body as organic forms of the flesh, but of the body in the psychology of those forms. How indeed could any meaning be immediately apparent when the body has such a perplexing way of portraying invisible matters where visibility is taken for granted?

This theme, the psychology of the body, touches on areas of interest which present unexpected difficulties. Every available aid towards the understanding of this subject is welcome. For that reason it belongs within this study of hysteria to digress momentarily from the main theme and to give undivided attention to the subject of body. For here, in the body and the mythic hole, lies the 'secret' of hysteria and the source of its unpredictable and deceptive presentations.

It is easy to overlook the fact that the visible flesh is but one expression of an otherwise invisible personality. Body and soul may belong together, but there is little doubt that they have undergone an intellectual separation into visible and invisible compartments where that of the soul is accorded the lesser reality. Seeds of misunderstanding thrive in this separation. The individual lives a delusion and the responses of a personality artificially divided into compartments in this manner are often discordant, if not confusing.

Moving from the living body to that of a sculptured nude gives a clearer view of how the psychology of the body is disrupted by this separation. The art of the sculptor presents the body as seen in a visual sense and also introduces its invisible idiom, leading effortlessly from an appreciation of what is seen towards more subtle contents. We may, for example, wonder when confronting Michaelangelo's *David*, Bernini's *Rape of Persephone* or Rodin's *Kiss* whether it is the body of an invisible image speaking from those pieces of marble, or whether it is really just that material body of marble itself. More simply, is the communication of art from the body of the image or the image of the body? The answer must surely be that they both speak. Marble alone is not enough.

From the meaning inherent in those sculpted works it begins to look as if body and image are in some way synonymous. The same phenomenon finds expression in the psychology of the living human body, though, as a result of the separation of body and soul into visible and invisible compartments, it is rarely recognised in this medium. The body now refers only to the matter of the flesh, while the image, if it means anything at all, is a vague and bodiless entity belonging to the invisible soul. A state has arisen in which it is difficult to appreciate the psyche in the visible body of the flesh, though its presence there is as real as that of the body in the image. As a result the very essence of the human body – an incomparably greater work of art than any marble statue – passes unrecognised.

The separation raises a difficulty for psychology. Body and image have inadvertently been divided in the same process that has divided body and soul. Yet an image takes its being from that of which it is an image; there can be no true division between them any more than between body and soul. The reflecting surface of the looking-glass lends confirmation to this fact: if I hold the glass in front of me, I am, whether I want it or not, imaged body and soul in the glass. But where is that image? It is certainly not in the looking-glass. Remove the glass and that fact is established. *On reflection* it becomes clear in what way and to what extent the image has a life, an existence of its own taking body from the body that it images. *Without reflection* the image, in spite of appearances, does not cease to be, but becomes indistinguishable from that which it images. In other words, with regard to the example, if the glass is taken away, I am no longer imaged, for I am myself the image.

It is true to say body and image are synonymous; they are reciprocating aspects of each other in that the image has life from the body while the body takes form from the image. Remarkable qualities inherent in the nature of image may indeed come to light on reflection, but not without the possibility of misunderstanding. A hazard of interpretation lies in the essential characteristic of likeness belonging to the image. There can be no image without likeness, but it is equally true to say that there *can* be likeness without an image. This is clearly apparent in the example of identical twins, where one is no more an image of the other than one brown egg is an image of another brown egg of similar dimensions. The likenesses are un-mistakable, but on reflection the true images come to light. When this concerns psychic images, especially in the practice of psycho-therapy, it is not always a simple task to see when there is an image and when there is merely a likeness. Reflection in the psychological meaning of the word is of paramount importance. A dream image may bear a striking likeness of, but is not an image of, the therapist.

It is, on the other hand, an image of the patient, who is unaware of the likeness and its significance.

Even if image and body prove to be aspects of each other, this still does not provide any satisfactory explanation of why Hades in the myth of Eleusis and silhouetted in that of hysteria makes a direct reference to the body. But that connection becomes clear with the reminder that Hades introduces the motif of death. No discussion on the body can be sufficient without it. Hades and the body may at first glance seem remote from each other, yet there is indeed an essential relationship and, if confirmation is needed, it becomes abundantly clear from two commonplace observations: that Hades is the Greek god of death and that death enters the world with the body and remains its constant companion throughout the span of life.

The emotional impact and the meaning of death for human existence, the terrors and the difficulties it brings to life, are alone enough to claim for it a role of central importance, not only in the Greek, but in all religions. The list of associated divinities is a long one; but from that list, Hades of ancient Greece remains comparatively close to contemporary culture, sharing features in common with the Devil of Christianity, the Prince of Death. To each is attributed a dwelling place in an underworld, though Hades has not undergone the separation of the Devil into a sovereign lord and a place of residence called Hell. Hades is both god and place. The Devil, on the other hand, has lost divinity and Hell is merely a residence. It is, therefore, easier to understand from the mythology of Hades rather than that of the Devil how death enters the world with the body. The birth of every child confirms this truth with the absolute certainty of the body's demise sooner or later.

The body may live, but it is bound to death for its very existence and meaning. At the inspiring moment of birth – an event which must surely reverberate throughout Hades, the hidden abode of death – we die into life as if, as the poet says, our life is but a sleeping and forgetting. The birth means that an image has taken body from Hades, has joined mortality and become subject to morbidity and open to disease. Death is not, as so often assumed, an antithesis of life, but a necessity for life's synthesis. That constant companion is the hidden force weaving the patterns of growth and decay which at times appear in the morbidities known as disease. Far from being the source of a catastrophic negation of life, death is a reminder that good health – if there is such a thing – is not an ideal state of freedom from disease, but a satisfactory way of adapting to the necessity of those diseases.

It must be apparent from this discussion on image and body that its significance does not lie simply in any photographic representation, but in the movements of life in which they participate. Likewise, Hades is not posing as an intellectual substitute for the Devil, but is a living myth. Talk of the image and body is also talk of the body and myth, for the imagery of myth, too, has body; it, too, can become visible in the flesh as, under other circumstances, it appears in the material of a sculpture. Thus Hades in the context of body and image is a theme with vitally important echoes throughout the whole field of medicine and disease, though it is to a large extent condemned to echo unheard in the noise of scientific research. At times the invisible movements of psychopathology find their mythic expression by establishing their presence in the flesh as organic disease.

This is by no means the accepted scientific understanding of illness, though none the less real for that oversight. Disease is for the most part understood only in terms of causes by external agents. If for any reason the agent is thought to lie within the constitution of the patient, that, too, is usually assumed to have been caused by external circumstances of the environment. The myth of disease, the diseased body as an expression of myth, is unrecognised. To put this in another way, disease as a necessary expression of the personality has lost its credibility and the whole field of medicine suffers the consequences of this depletion.

Confirming the necessity of regarding disease as myth as well as a physical syndrome is that Hades is also known as the 'Son of Chronos with so many Names', one of which is 'He Who receives so Many'. This much feared and respected divinity was also widely venerated as Pluto, a name associated with riches. Pluto, as the ruler of the underworld, is a divine figure who reciprocates with the tides of life and death in the way that death receives buried treasures from the earth and so holds riches for life. The riches originating in the earth – matter, body and disease – are bestowed as gifts on living creatures, but are such that they have an unwelcome ring for those who are blind to the spirituality of death. They are many in number. If death is understood only in terms of predicting an ultimate demise, there can be little chance of realising that death has already arrived. It is as an outcome of that limited horizon that casual references to death are mostly heard in terms of his or her death, my death, your death, as if death were a personal possession. The 'riches' it provides, manifesting in and through the body, pass unnoticed largely because of their immediate bearing on the patterns of disease and healing. This unfamiliar aspect of disease as psychic necessity is one where myth brings as much, if not more, understanding than the microscope. Its importance cannot be too strongly emphasised for, although it may not be the immediate concern of curing, it is the immediate concern of movements in healing and the medium through which disease brings meaning and fulfilment to the life of its victims.

But what of death in relation to hysteria? The message conveyed by the motif is clearly that death is not just the business of the undertaker but, in this context, the very subject matter of the physician and psychotherapist. Virtually no disease has escaped some encounter with hysteria in the course of its long history. It is the quality of likeness to these disorders that leaves behind it the perennial question: what is the nature of this disease? Is it or is it not an illness in its own right? Death with regard to hysteria is the key figure leading directly to the source of hysteric deception and misunderstanding.

Of recent years these questions have arisen less often in the field of purely physical medicine, but more intensely in that of psychosomatic disorders and the neuroses, the place where hysteria found its most comfortable and effective home. This latest scene provides excellent material to pursue the theme of death and its significance in the body in respect of hysteria. Writer's or musician's cramp, for example, is a pathological state presenting physical symptoms in the body more immediately and more understandably connected with unconscious psychic conflict than many other and better known ailments. Here the question arises: what is the nature of this crippling spasm that presents without an organic cause? Is it a neurosis or is it a conversion hysteria? And if it is hysteria, why is it not psycho-somatic?

There is some confusion of meaning amongst these familiar terms of psychopathology, especially between neurotic and psychosomatic illness. To differentiate at least hysteria within the imbroglio by giving attention to its myth is a considerable step towards clarity and even towards ending a lax and unreflected use of the other terms. All the disorders mentioned make their appearance in the body. This might be assumed to be the one reliable feature, yet the body is the place where much confusion and misunderstanding lie. We talk knowingly of a healthy body and a sick body, of a sensitive or an athletic, even of a neurotic body. Is there perhaps such a thing as an hysteric body? The term does not appear officially in medical textbooks, though some might say it is deserving of greater recognition than it receives. The notion suggests an apt way to confront the question of conversions and psychosomatic disorders.

9

THE BUSINESS OF A NOBODY

The whole field of hysteria lies in a twilight darkness where the paths are poorly lit and the signposts unreliable. It is easy to mistake the way. As a precautionary measure for this discussion, the choice of the word 'hysteric' rather than 'hysterical' needs some comment lest it be the cause of a misunderstanding. Both these adjectives are accepted in the larger dictionaries and are freely used in conversation. It is probable, but by no means certain, that for most people they convey the same meaning.

The word 'hysteric' is an adjective derived from the medical term hysteria, after the same manner that manic comes from mania and paraplegic from paraplegia. The word 'hysterical', on the other hand, has the questionable right of being an adjective derived from the adjective hysteric. 'Hysteric' is descriptive of the disease hysteria, whereas it seems likely that 'hysterical' is loosely applied to people or situations conveying a picture of uncontrolled emotionality with extravagant theatrical behaviour. The venerable disease hysteria is much more than highly emotional behaviour and its adjective hysteric is, certainly in medical circles, not limited to that feature.

In her book *The Second Sex* Simone de Beauvoir refers to the hysteric body, though it must be put on record that in translation it appears as the hysteric*al* body. Following the definitions suggested above, it seems probable from her description that the word 'hysteric' was intended. But in either case, it serves to mask one prevalent misunderstanding of hysteria that has pestered its movements with great persistence through the centuries. She writes, 'the body of woman – particularly that of a young girl – is an hysterical body in the sense that there is, so to speak, no distance between psychic life and its physiological realisation' (p. 311). This is a revealing contribution to psychology. There is much truth in the statement, though it says less about the 'second sex' than about the psychology of the body. In the context in which it appears, that truth would have been greater if the word 'hysterical' had been omitted and some other adjective substituted. Although the sentence appears in a setting where it may be excused from a literal exactness, it is impossible to overlook the implication of an insult; if woman's body, young or old, is in any way hysteric, it must follow as a logical assumption that natural woman is tainted with disease. Clearly no such meaning is intended, even though there has always been the tendency to equate woman with hysteria. As it stands, the statement shows the disadvantage of introducing the theme of hysteria without precise meaning. It is generally accepted, physiologically and psychologically, that woman's relation to the body differs to that of man; but that body is not therefore diseased or hysteric. The term 'emotionally responsive' might with advantage replace the misleading word 'hysteric', though the real meaning of the sentence remains simply that woman's body is womanly.

What then is the hysteric body if not that of a woman? An answer must lie somewhere in the realms of psychopathology and without much prospect of an easy search, bearing in mind that the kindred psychopathology is in the likeness of a hole in a psychic image. That hole would leave an empty space wide open to distortion from projections were it not for one feature, already noted, that may save it from misrepresentation: it is not exactly an empty, formless lacuna in that it is the silhouette of a specific content. The hole is, as it were, an image without body. Is the hole saying simply that hysteria is no more than the fanciful life of every daydreamer from the nursery to the mad house who is guided by the illusion of insubstantial fantasy? Not quite; there is more to hysteria than living out idle, bodiless fantasies. A look at the situation conveyed through two specific myths will corroborate that denial, for it says that body, death and disease are akin to each other and that hysteria's connection with them is not convincing. There is in fact something convincing and real about hysteria, but not where it concerns the body. At any moment hysteria may surprise with the reality of its pathology and yet still fail to be the disease it seems.

From this discussion and the reflections it casts on the hysteric body, one important and convincing feature emerges: hysteria is a silhouette of disease. The myth implies that hysteria is not a real disease or, as previously noted, is more than is generally understood by the term 'illness'. Nevertheless hysteria exists very close to disease; it seems in fact to flirt with disease and is largely dependent on this mode of relationship for definition. Witness the indecision of physicians through the ages when confronted with hysteria as a differential diagnosis.

To accept that hysteria is not a real disease is, to say the least, a disconcerting predicament for all physicians, the custodians of illness. Speaking of disease where none is present, as they have done through the centuries with regard to hysteria, suggests that those physicians are victims of a deception. To a certain extent that claim is true, though it cannot be grounds for serious embarrassment when bearing in mind that the ability to deceive is essential to the nature of hysteria and that this deception belongs rightly in the field of medicine. It cannot altogether be classed as a mistake; but deception, none the less, is a characteristic that radiates mistrust and suspicion to a point that presses for satisfaction. In the context of the hysteric body and its relation to disease that means a look at the theme of hysteria and malingering. After that the discussion moves to other fields; to neurosis and psychosomatic disorders as prominent examples of disease never far removed from hysteria.

Malingering is an old disease. No one can say exactly when the awareness of doubt regarding the motives of their patients first entered the minds of physicians as being a significant feature of the pathology; but it is known that Hippocratic physicians of ancient Greece were aware of a need to distinguish between epileptic and hysteric convulsions. Why the differential diagnosis carried such importance was for the good reason that mistrust was around; hysteria, then as now, carried the suspicion of malingering. Disease, it seems, has always fostered dishonesty as well as discomfort. What other motif would prompt anyone to present a known disease without the accepted organic cause unless it were to deceive?

Malingering, viewed as a form of disease, may be open to question, but it is important enough to claim a history in the field of medicine. When in the sixteenth century the Dutch physician, J. Weyer (1515–88), wrote on malingering, he did not, like many of those before and after him, equate it with hysteria. Superstitious and demonic diseases existed beside established organic ailments, making difficulties for diagnosis, but Weyer was quick to recognise genuine mental illness and distinguish it from the fraudulent practices of malingering. It must have been this sensitivity to the presence of fraud that led him to go against popular opinion at the time of witch hunting and exonerate some 'hysteric' women. Weyer was one of the few to declare that not all those convicted were to blame for their misdemeanours; that there were unfortunate, often lonely, women in the world who became the innocent victims of other women who were accomplices of the Devil. Their actions as a result were not wholly intentional and they could not be held responsible for their sinful state or for the crimes they were said to commit as a result of this victimisation. At its worst this state could only be a passive sort of witchery: some form of illness rather than a sin, and at the same time not fraudulent.

Weyer's work was a valuable contribution to human rights and at the same time an intimation that hysteria, even if considered to be a mortal sin rather than a disease, was none the less drastically different from the sin of fraudulence. Three hundred years later the American neurologist, Weir Mitchell (1829–1914), made a study of casualties in the American Civil War with similar intent, to exonerate certain victims of wrong diagnosis. His researches were directed towards the theme of deception in disease, and they concerned specifically three pathologies: organic nervous injuries, hysteria and malingering. The pivot of this work, the feature that touched directly on the problem of hysteria and malingering, was his recognition of the state of 'nostalgia', a form of homesickness in the army that had a dangerous influence on the reactions of military authorities to the wounds and illnesses suffered by their soldiers. Nostalgia was, according to Mitchell, a state closely allied to malingering, but even closer to hysteria. He wrote of his regret, 'that no careful study was made of what was in some instances an interesting psychic malady (nostalgia), making man hysteric and incurable except by discharge (from the army)' (Veith 1965, p. 214). Nostalgia was not the simple dishonesty of a calculated deception but an emotional state akin to hysteria.

Malingering and hysteria share in common the ability to attract strong moral disapproval and, because of that, an inappropriate or misplaced interest. Malingering achieves this because it is known to be a deliberate deception, and hysteria because it is assumed to be deliberate; but such righteous indignation misses the point. It gets in the way, clouds the picture and unconsciously confuses the two. As a result of the squandered energies, the two states do not receive sufficient differentiation as a feature of pathology and, lacking discrimination, are unconsciously, or subconsciously, paired together even when known intellectually to differ radically from each other. Yet, in spite of popular prejudice, always ready to assume that the state of hysteria is a consciously contrived disease, all the personalities of note and influence in medicine have, like Weir Mitchell, been of the opinion that hysteria and malingering, though they both display deception, are different pathologies.

The question is, if these two disorders are essentially two forms of deception, how do they differ? In the case of hysteria, the need to deceive is to a greater extent a self-deception than a deception of others. The same cannot be said of malingering. Mitchell made this clear with his interest in nostalgia. He had the benefit of nineteenth-century psychiatry and the beginnings of depth psychology to help him see how nostalgia, like hysteria, presents a lowered and diminished field of consciousness; an *abaissement du niveau mental* (as Jung calls it after Pierre Janet) with a greater than average susceptibility to suggestion from both inside and out. If in nostalgia or hysteria the influence of auto-suggestion is not recognised or respected, the effects may well be judged a calculated fraudulence and mistaken for malingering. The two states can be deceptively similar. They are easily confused with each other even though the quality of consciousness, as well as the conscious intent, differ considerably. Witch hunting exemplifies this dangerous borderline to good effect: how many of those who died would have bothered to malinger knowing that the penalty for discovery was burning at the stake?

In contrast to those of hysteria, the undertakings of malingering are heroic and function with a bright, clear-cut quality of consciousness. It is rarely encountered in a pure form, or at least not for long, for the strains imposed on the malingerer are severe and the ability to maintain the level of conscious attention necessary to deceive is limited accordingly. The most surprising of the differences between these two conditions lies in the psychology of the body. Even if the flesh is mutilated deliberately, the effects of malingering within the body are relatively small. Indeed, how could they be otherwise when the motivation is consciously fraudulent? Yet those effects, though small, must be judged greater than in the case of hysteria. And why is that? Because the malingerer's fraudulent practices are the outcome of a substantial and an active imagination which, for better or for worse, brings some movement of transformation in the personality, and so in the body, on all levels of understanding of that word. Hysteria in itself cannot claim this degree of movement. Both may demonstrate some involvement of the physical body, but whereas the pathology of hysteria evokes an exaggerated importance, that of malingering is marked with the psychic reality of a disease, although it is not taken seriously as such. Malingering has a far greater pathological effect on the individual than might be expected. That aspect of the condition is largely overlooked in practice.

The quality of the conscious intent makes differentiation of hysteria from malingering a relatively simple matter. A more demanding exercise is to grasp the essential difference between hysteria and psychosomatic disorders. From the many examples of hysteria open to choice, one is particularly suitable for discussion, combining as it does a visible somatic ailment together with a strong psychic component. This is 'conversion hysteria', a term used by Freud to define one category of the psychoneuroses. The symptoms are mildly fantastic and well suited to the popular idea of what hysteria should be, to the extent that conversion really is hysteria for many people while all other manifestations are open to doubt. Freud explained by way of a sexual aetiology the translation of affect into the body as a physical ailment. He maintained that the symptoms bear symbolic significance and that, when they appear, there is an absence of anxiety. As a term of diagnosis, conversion hysteria entered quickly into the vocabulary of medicine but has recently undergone modification. The name has been changed to that of 'conversion symptom' and the syndrome divorced from sexuality and all ties with hysteria.

In the context of body psychopathology this illness demonstrates another area of confused identity where hysteria stands true to its characteristic tendency to dim every border it touches. Conversion hysteria shares with all neurotic disorders the absence of an organic cause, but this it does in a singular manner that seems to go out of its way to prove that there can be no possibility of organic cause. It needs the skills of a trained physician to detect the diagnostic signs that distinguish this form of hysteria from organic nervous or muscular lesions. The specialist's knowledge shows that the physical disorders follow an anatomical pattern corresponding more with the patient's than the physician's idea of how the body works. Anaesthesia or paralysis cover a symbolic 'glove and stocking' area of the limbs rather than irregular details in the pattern of an actual nerve distribution unknown to the patient. It is a strange illness indeed that can so abuse the very meaning of anatomical fact and function and yet be real and genuine in as much as it is not a demonstration of malingering. Only the nature of its anatomical inaccuracy leaves it open to a suspicion of duplicity.

Freud described in a stimulating as well as convincing way how the syndrome is both a physical and a psychic disorder. Why then is it understood as hysteria rather than a psychosomatic disease? The various forms in which hysteria present are, if not with the downright

101

deception of malingering, often not without a suspicion of mistrust. But then, psychosomatic illness is, too, not always convincing in its presentations or, more accurately, physicians are not always clear about the meaning of the terms they use. The subject has never been an easy one to follow. That mental illness can be the cause of, but also the result of, organic disorder has been recognised certainly since the time of Galen. Psychosomatic medicine, on the other hand, has appeared only in this century; but in spite of this newly discovered and expanding branch of medicine, the reciprocal functions of body and mind in the aetiology of disease remain as obscure and as far apart as ever.

The ambiguous nature of causality in psychosomatic illness makes it a highly controversial entity. Dictionaries are disappointing in that definitions are for the most part formulated in terms of a body and mind duality with emphasis on the mind as the moving factor. Such explanations must be inadequate. They describe only the basis of all so-called psychogenic illness, and that would include hysteria. Indeed, as all somatic illness must include some psychic factor, most attempts at the definition of psychosomatic illness are unconvincing. The endeavours produce an unwieldy but vaguely understood spectrum which could theoretically embrace anything from cancer to a common cold. Probably as an outcome of this uncertainty the number of officially recognised individual items of psychosomatic disease was until recently small. The influence of psychology brings greater possibilities of definition and a more rewarding picture. Here they have been described as disturbances of an image that involves the body or, more comprehensively, of body images as a whole. This approach touches on a more satisfying line of thought even if the formulations are still vague.

Anatomy and physiology have contributed much to establishing psychosomatic medicine, though not enough towards understanding its nature. The part played by the autonomic nervous system in the transmission of emotion is of central importance in localising sites of disease, but it has needed depth psychology to confirm the psychosomatic relevance. Following the work of C. G. Jung and others in psychogalvanometry and that of Freud in the field of psychoneurosis, came an explanation of psychosomatic disease as an organic disturbance produced by way of the autonomic nervous system. Conversion hysteria, on the other hand, followed a distribution of the central nervous system. There is much truth in it. Typically, conversion hysteria does indeed appear as paralysis or anaesthesia in the limbs, whilst psychosomatic illness typically involves the internal organs; but there can be no escaping the fact that hysteric disease through the centuries has been known to involve internal organs as well as the limbs and trunk. How does this contradiction fit into the picture?

It is often said about medical practice in the past that many of the organic diseases in question would in all probability not have been diagnosed as hysteria today. There is much to support that assumption; nevertheless it is an evasion of the truth and not a valid argument, for it overlooks the nature of hysteria. Whatever diagnosticians may say now, the ailments so diagnosed *were* hysteria in those days and, if hysteria is to be taken seriously, they must be understood as such. These were not the mistakes of scientific ignorance, but careful records of hysteric disease. The criticism of diagnostic procedures in the past is a reflection only on hysteria as it is today. Yet, in spite of the enlightenments born of contemporary skills, the same tangle still exists, for there can be little doubt that many symptoms of conversion do still involve internal organs as well as the limbs as, for example, in hysteric vomiting, fainting and diarrhoea.

A precise differentiation between the two pathologies can be a taxing exercise. An addition to the difficulties is the fact that psychosomatic and hysteric disorders may be present at the same time, may even overflow into each other. Differentiation is none the less a necessary requirement for prescribing appropriate treatment.

Signs and symptoms may be misleading, but one fundamental fact of great clarity is there to guide the understanding: hysteric and psychosomatic disorders are expressions of different myths. It does not make the diagnosis, but it influences the thinking of anyone confronted with the problem of differentiation. The myth of hysteria reflects a state that might, yet does not, have psychic body, meaning that, in terms of psychopathology, the disorder is in itself genuine, but not in the way that it seems to be; that the condition is disturbing, but primarily because of the hysteric symptom complex; that it is theatrical in presentation, but superficial and ineffective in its transforming potential. The hysteric ailments are not symptoms of disease in the body, but of passing demonstrations through the body. In contrast, psychosomatic disturbances differ in the sense that they reflect archetypal patterns which involve the body. As an understanding of the psychosomatic factor arises directly from the place of the hysteric hole, it might be tempting, but quite erroneous, to assume that the myth of Eleusis is by contrast the image of psychosomatic illness. Every archetypal image expressed in myth has its psychopathology, but that is not the concern of the moment. The relevance of the myth in this context lies in the outline it brings to the nature of hysteria and not in any specific pathology it might otherwise define. The pathologies confirm how psychosomatic illness, unlike hysteria, is a psychic experience of the body that, as it were, touches and moves the soul.

Psychosomatic disorders are slow to appear, born of remote and longlasting psychic conflicts ultimately protesting their emotions in the body, not as passing demonstrations, but as disease. The severity of the disorder beside that of conversion hysteria is in proportion to the psychic remoteness, the inaccessibility and the compulsion of the conflict – factors often not recognised in the over-enthusiastic practice of analytic therapists who assume their approach is the specific cure of choice. Hysteric conversion, on the other hand, breaks upon the scene suddenly and is usually, though not invariably, of relatively short duration. In comparison the conflict is nearer to consciousness and more available for recognition, as Freud confirmed in the reductive ways of psychoanalysis. The two states that sometimes seem so similar are poles apart. Psychosomatic illness may kill, but may also transform its victims, while the hysteric conversion, if present alone and not confused with another syndrome of disease, neither kills nor touches the depths.

The distinction between hysteria and psychosomatics may be convincing as far as it goes, but there remains a question of central importance which can no longer be overlooked. What is the nature of relations between hysteria and neurosis when the psychoneurosis of conversion is itself referred to as hysteria?

A little appreciated characteristic of hysteria is the mediumistic manner in which it senses and participates in what is 'in the air'. In its own particular way it plays a significant part in the changing forms of culture, as if it were always on the spot with an antenna like that of the famous fashion houses or leaders of society; but always hysteria is near the fashion of psychopathology. It was, as already noted, especially prominent during the religious unrest that spread from heretic to hysteric witch hunting and was again particularly noticeable in the cultural scene of medicine at the time of the Enlightenment. There can therefore be little surprise to find hysteria involved in the affairs of neurosis after that category of disorder appeared in the eighteenth century. Prior to this discovery, hysteria had established a reputation for changing appearances, but with the arrival of neurosis and the growing study of psychology, came a strong movement towards identifying hysteria as an homogeneous disease. Why that should happen at this point in history is more than pure chance and probably connected with the fact that the short history of neurosis shares much in common with that of its older colleague, hysteria. Both had a propensity for change and both ultimately lost their status as a recognised individual item of disease. Is it possible that neurosis is but a modern, sophisticated name for hysteria or is this one more episode in the history of hysteria dimming the borders it touches? In other words, is neurosis merely hysteria or is it a category of disease that became infected more severely than others by hysteria?

After two centuries neurosis remains an uncertain quantity and, like hysteria, most people know what it is as long as they are not asked. The forms neurosis may take are legion. The intention here is not to wrestle with problems of definition, but suffice it to say that in a random choice from an Adlerian organic inferiority, a Jungian crisis in the second half of life or a Freudian psychoneurosis, the movements of disease are present in the claims of primordial images playing out their myth in the body, apparently without consideration for the havoc wrought on the life of the patient. That is to say, neurosis is a severe disturbance in that it, like a psychosomatic illness, touches the body as a moving and potentially transforming experience. Though it is not, like its psychosomatic counterpart, a direct threat to life, it takes a rightful place amongst the other diseases constituting the field of illness precisely because neurosis is *not* hysteria. A moment's reflection confirms the body's involvement; it may appear as the visible, physical state of a neurasthenic collapse or as a conversion symptom or as a fixed yet invisible debility of severe psychoneurosis which patients experience vaguely, but convincingly, in the physical body. This leads to the phenomenon of conversion and the last question for the differentiation of hysteria in matters of the body.

If, as already stated, neurosis takes its place in the field of disease but is not hysteria, it must of necessity follow that the authenticity of conversion hysteria is open to doubt. Is that, too, excluded from its field? A 'glove and stocking' or any pattern of conversion classified by Freud as a psychoneurosis is anatomically incorrect and may be little more than a relatively harmless alteration in the flesh, but it is undeniably a psychic reality registering its presence (symbolically, as Freud said) in the body. The paralysed hand may not in fact be true paralysis of the hand, but it is a symbolic expression of that image, whereas hysteria, with whatever symptoms it may present, does not belong psychologically to that or any other specific image of disease. It means that conversion manifests in the body like any other disease, may be classed correctly as a neurosis, but is not in itself hysteria. This was confirmed by the medical profession when the name of the disorder was changed from 'conversion hysteria' to 'conversion symptom'.

The question arose while reflecting on death, disease and Hades whether there is such a thing as an hysteric body. The question now is whether this inquiry into the psychosomatics of illness throws light on the subject matter. Any unequivocal statements on a topic of this nature are unlikely to carry conviction; but this much is moderately clear: the short discussion on malingering, psychosomatic disease and neurosis establishes their transforming potential through the body and their reality as disease in contrast to the simulation of hysteria. Even the neurosis of conversion proves not to be a simple hysteria simulation, but a form of neurotic illness in its own right. This knowledge suggests that an hysteric body has the nature of an image without body – a doubtful, ambiguous and even slightly ostentatious-sounding description. It may hold some meaning for the depth psychologist, but is without relevance in most other walks of life. This prompts the question whether there is in fact such a thing as an image without body. Probably not; and yet that symbolic expression does bring a glimmer of meaning to something beyond description – the bodily frame carrying within it an insubstantial image; an emotionality within, yet not of, the body, highly suggestible, but unrelated; a whirling of movement without effect. Whatever form it takes, the presence of the hysteria is an outline only and without the substance of body to facilitate transformation.

The hysteric body is a 'no-body'. No disrespect is implied in that observation, for those heavily imbued with hysteric characteristics are familiar with the subjective difficulties this complaint may present. Hysteria, where it concerns pathology, draws attention to disease through simulation. On its withdrawal from the scene – often abrupt and disconcerting – an untarnished picture of the disease remains; a pathology of image and body is revealed. The same pattern has disconcerting subjective effects on those who are markedly hysteric. At one moment there is a confident, clear understanding of a situation; at the next that confidence has disappeared and self-awareness diminished to the deranged feeling of being 'nobody'. But just here lies the essential psychological value of the suggestibility, for withstanding the unpleasant threat of losing one's sense of being leaves one's real being unhampered. There is the possiblity of more lasting confidence and an unexpected originality of functioning.

The hysteric body may present difficulties for so-called norms of behaviour, but it is also a treasure of originality and an instrument of individuation. As the advantages are less often recognised than the difficulties it can be no wonder that an imprecise use of the word 'hysteria' has such popular appeal as a vaguely excusable, but none the less effective, term of disapproval.

10

HELP AT ALL COSTS

For over 3,000 years hysteria played an active part in pathology before any official classification of disease began a serious threat to deny its existence. Many unsuccessful attempts had been made to pin down hysteria as an individual item of disease, so that some were glad to be rid at last of this embarrassment to medical science. Others were surprised, even shocked, that such a venerable disease could be so lightly dismissed, apparently because a few physicians thought it did not exist. A few were indifferent to the news and, undeterred by the event, continued to work in their different ways with the unfinished story of hysteria.

These essays have approached hysteria by way of myth and meaning rather than by the more familiar medical paths of symptomatic facts and findings. Myth not only assumes, but even confirms the existence of hysteria, yet not with any categorical denial of recent medical decisions. This is a very telling feature. It may seem like a contradiction in that any support of the medical opinion would be to agree with the non-existence of hysteria; but that is only a part of the picture. The myth confirms the existence, but at the same time confirms that hysteria is not what it seems to be. For often it seems to be a disease. To say that hysteria is not a disease does not deny it the right of existence. It merely leaves the more difficult problem of establishing what it is. If some distinctive features have already come to light, others will follow as long as hysteria is not approached as if it must be a disease.

There is no doubt that the events of recent history have diminished the importance of clinical facts and findings in the study of hysteria. Time moves on, the cultural scene changes and the foremost place of involvement is no longer in symptoms and signs. Hysteria now appears as prominently in the treatment as in earlier times it did in the course of disease. This is noticeable especially, though not exclusively, in the many different practices of psychotherapy. That branch of therapeutics more than others is a model of hysteric infection.

Hysteria's participation in therapeutics is not new; the present scene is merely a concentration of what has gone before. The characteristics are in every respect similar to those found previously in the causes and presentations of disease. Strong emotionality, deception, some dissociation and, above all, exaggeration are all there, making the realities of therapy not quite what they seem to be. This present choice of venue was foreseeable in so far as hysteria has always shown an affinity with the psyche or the psychological aspect of whatever it touched. As the part it played in the portrayal of disease no longer carries its erstwhile conviction, the place of psyche in therapeutics is the natural selection, if only for hysteria to complete its participation in the dictum of myth, that like causes and cures like; the same god sends and heals the disease. If hysteria appears in one it will appear in the other and, whatever the contribution it has made to pathology, it will make a corresponding one to treatment.

There are many aspects from which to view the field of therapeutics and each in its own way – collective and personal – reflects the influence of hysteria. One of these is to consider the overall picture that this branch of medicine presents. An explosive outburst has taken place in the second half of the twentieth century, swelling the numbers of therapists in all departments of their work and extending the boundaries of medicine into unexpected territories. Although the intentions are for the most part highly commendable, the effects bear the unmistakable imprint of hysteria. The theatrical element is strong and with it there is not only a desire, but a rush to be in the spotlight at all costs. Every conceivable sort of 'fringe' practice – especially in the field of psychotherapy – is available on the market; indeed not even on the market, but often bestowed gratis on any takers. They gather their converts with the speed of pseudo-religious conversions at a revivalist meeting. California alone must have produced as many new psychotherapies in as short a time as it has varieties of religious sects; other countries follow close behind. The earnest approach of Freud's psychoanalysis and related methods of analysing the psyche for therapeutic purposes have given way to other sorts of weekly programmes, supplemented by family therapies, partner therapies and many other forms of counselling, ways of meditation and variations on Yoga practice, dance and movement therapies, astrological therapies, autogenous training and many more. A vast assortment from primal screams to reincarnations is available to fill the week and somehow it all manages to squeeze under the umbrella of the magic word 'psychotherapy'.

Glancing at this list, the quantity alone is suspicious. It lures the participants into taking it all for granted. Psychotherapy in one form or another has broken out and spreads like an infectious disease or – more appropriately – like hysteria. In fact it is not too much to say an 'hysterical gold-rush' has transformed the whole field of therapeutics into a caricature of its former self. It functions through the attitude that anyone can do psychotherapy, and in this way offers an occupation for the unfulfilled rather than a vocational necessity. It is on a wave of popularity coinciding in a marked way with devaluation of hysteria in the field of pathology.

Fascination with the practice of therapeutics has spread beyond the interests of the profession. The possibilities have captivated many who cannot be said to do more than dabble in their new pastime, albeit with the best of intentions. To say the least, the present situation, especially with regard to psychotherapy, has suffered a dubious proliferation that brings to mind the word 'exaggeration'. The enthusiasm it has aroused is of dangerous proportions and quite inappropriate for a work of such sober needs. There is hysteria in this picture, mocking it with a warning notice to say that it is not what it seems to be, yet with the added reminder that there is an important reality within this extravagant, emotional demonstration. The influence of this remarkable phenomenon on therapeutics may be judged from a look at specific areas of hysteria's intervention.

Wherever the subject of therapeutics arises the operative word is 'healing'. The two are so nearly synonymous that healing is taken for granted in all practices of therapy. This amounts to the same thing as saying that healing is taken for granted in all prescriptions of treatment. For therapeutics is clearly the province of treatment. Hearing these self-evident observations on healing may make no immediate impression, yet the implications they hold concern the fate of many unsatisfactory features surrounding the practice and administration of medical services today. There is some mis-understanding attached to healing.

Though healing and the practice of therapeutics are aspects of the same thing, when the familiar term treatment is used, the operative word in the generally accepted use of that term is not healing, but curing. Does this mean that healing is the same as curing? That question opens up a different aspect of the subject. To many it may seem like splitting hairs; yet differentiation between healing and curing is of great importance if misundertandings are to be avoided. They are not the same thing; furthermore, the border between the two is especially unclear where hysteria exerts its influence for better or for worse.

Treatment to remove the cause and to effect the cure follows a pattern as old as the history of medicine. Of necessity, it covers a complex field and has changed in its ways as much as the science to which it is attached. It is at the same time true to say that treatment, as that word is understood today, does not stretch much further back than the beginning of the twentieth century. The ways of curing disease have changed dramatically in the last hundred years to be hardly recognisable beside those of former times. Sensational scien-tific achievements have altered the face of medicine, bringing many advantages for ailing human beings. Such is the tale of achievement that it comes as a surprise to realise that cures still do not match up to the unqualified successes they are thought, or assumed, to be. Indeed, in the face of such success, it is not easy to see what is amiss. Near miracles are available and presumed, yet disapproval and dissatisfaction are the outcome of the chase for perfect health. There can be little doubt that exaggeration in various forms permeates all areas of curing. It lies in the way cures are advertised and it lies in the demands of the public. Suggestibility where therapeutics are concerned is at its height.

Cure for disease has always carried high hopes, though whether it has always carried the expectations of certain solution for all illness, as it does today, is not so sure. Certainly since the work of Louis Pasteur in the nineteenth century (at the time when hysteria was enjoying a most prominent role), this attitude is increasingly prevalent. That great French chemist and research worker is justly famous for his discovery of the anthrax bacillus and for grounding the study of bacteriology which paved the way for the wider discovery of bacteria as the cause of disease. Inevitably, the search for cures intensified and led ultimately to antibiotics and a series of miraculous discoveries in the 1930s long since stripped of their grandeur and taken for granted. This development brought a compelling, but premature, authority to the role of curing. The power available and the sense of achievement through the use of antibiotics are dangerous experiences; they lend themselves to a hubris culminating in the vague idea that there is a possibility at hand to eliminate illness altogether. With science reigning supreme, it has only to fight and conquer those external agents that cause disease and all will be well.

Fashions change. Bacteria have to some extent been exposed, have yielded up their secrets and lost glamour to the virus, which is even smaller and still holds secrets. The virus is in vogue to explain the cause of unknown illness; but not without competition. Its popularity has been challenged by the role of biochemistry, which has recently become a sensational and a focal point in the mechanics of disease and now carries many of the responsibilities previously attributed to bacteria. 'Diet' is the cure.

It is not the object of this essay to discuss the causes of disease, but to emphasise the prevalent qualities of exaggeration and instability around the expectations of cure. The actual achievements in this field are in themselves magnificent, but they are obliged to function in a deceptive form of isolation. Curing has lost the co-operation of healing and hysteria has a considerable influence on that dissociation.

As already stated, for those who undertake the psychotherapeutic care of human souls, the operative word is 'healing'. The topic is one of vital importance and maintains one of the few remaining links between the practice of medicine and that of religion from which medicine took origin. In both fields the word 'healing' is accepted and used as definitive of their central purpose. Yet this is not an easily definable area, is troublesome for scientific explanation and mystifying for everything else. The subject of healing is shrouded in obscurity, where it receives a large amount of enthusiasm but a marked lack of attention; furthermore, the border it shares with curing is dim and differentiation is diffcult. The result is that misunderstandings arise, one of which leads to a misappropriation of the word 'healing'.

What does healing mean? The word comes from close association with 'hale', meaning 'whole'. From here healing has grown to mean curing disease, whereas its truer meaning is 'making whole'. Just this most admirable intent of making whole is where unsuspected misunderstanding is likely to undermine the process, both in religious and medical practices.

Where healing is the concern of the Church, the role of God assumes greater importance and is more pressing than in medicine. It is certainly the realm where healing might best be understood, for whether that understanding is in terms of theology or of other approaches, this supernatural phenomenon is beyond the will-power and capabilities of conscious intent. In matters of transcendance, the religious calling of the Church should theoretically have a big advantage; yet healing remains even more vague and deceptive in these well-intentioned hands than it does in those of physicians, for no better reason than that it is confused with curing while the supernatural side is taken for granted.

It is readily understandable that differentiation is no easy task, for essentially healing and curing belong together. They do not require separation, but they do require a clear appreciation that they are not one and the same. That is the point where misunderstanding arises to undermine and dilute the authority of psychotherapy by taking the psyche out of the therapy. As there is always a psychic component to be found in any experience, it may well be argued that there is an element of psychotherapy in anything from psycho-analysis to prescribing an aspirin. That broad view contains an element of truth; it is simple to understand, but it may be used as justification for any form of treatment to be accepted as psycho-therapy. On the one hand it acknowledges the presence and import-ance of a psychic factor, while on the other it makes a mockery of psychotherapy which, for all its youthfulness, has established a place of professional importance and respect. Psychotherapy cannot be expected to embrace any form of treatment aiming to help the patient. In fact a large part of the work done under the heading of psychotherapy may be more accurately defined as psychonursing. If the observation sounds demeaning, let it be said at once that the intended work is none the worse for that definition. There is no derogatory implication, unless the practice is passing deliberately for what it is not.

Most of the recognised cures prescribed are efficacious and, on the whole, good in themselves. They represent an essential feature in the 'art of healing', though it is doubtful if that term is still appropriate. The overall approach to illness has changed so much that therapeutic administration is realised only as a craft applied as if it were itself the healing rather than an art that touches on healing. But wholeness and healing are something to get in touch with, not something to be made. Many of those who practise therapeutics are unaware of this truth and so of an art in their work. They equate healing with the relief of suffering and elimination of tension, though this is by no means necessarily the case. No one would dispute the value or deny the praiseworthy intention, but at the same time, it is doubtful whether the effects of the practice are synonymous with the movements of healing. Indeed the good intentions may inadvertently hinder those movements by failing to take into consideration the needs rather than the wishes of the patient, the psychological necessity and the basic premise on which healing rests.

A wound in the flesh sets in motion the movements of healing; not those of curing. Numerous different applications are available as cures for wounds of all sorts and are designed with intent to facilitate healing. No microscope can ever reveal the whole wondrous picture, for it needs a study of the psyche to probe further into those invisible areas where an autonomous, self-regulated process of healing takes place. It is a study around an area of mystery; a source of endless interest and importance, which includes recognition of the natural healing process as well as the psychic factor involved in that process and facilitated by the presence of a psychotherapist. Analytic therapists know this under the heading of 'transference', a phenomenon belonging in the realm of cure, but central to the art of healing. Freud described this phenomenon of transference in detail and Jung extended this to include the dimension of autonomous, archetypal psychic movement that gives credence to art in the psychotherapy.

On the contemporary scene the field of therapeutics is everywhere carried on a wave of hysteria, subject to hypersuggestibility and caught in a frenzy of enthusiasm of blinding proportions. It is even subject to an hysteric dissociation in the way the upsurge of curing functions in isolation and relatively dissociated from the living roots of healing. This is the pattern of the hysteric silhouette, of the image without body, wherein the work of curing does not touch the substance of healing and, in fact, only seems to be achieving those transformations attributed to it.

These reflections on the overall picture of therapeutics and the deceptions hysteria fosters in that field say little about its influence on the practitioners or on those who are the recipients of their practice. What is happening to these custodians of cure that causes them to overlook the presence of healing?

Therapists of all sorts are part of that body known as the helping professions, and the help is, as it were, the moth that finds itself drawn irresistibly towards the flame of hysteria. Help, that eminently desirable Christian virtue may pass without question under almost any circumstances other than those of serious psychotherapy; but here there are grounds for reservations. When the psyche is taken seriously, when it is recognised and respected in a manner fitting for an encounter with the soul, the subject of help becomes ambiguous. The work demands a standard of awareness beyond that of many enthusiastic helpers who, unaware of the shadow their good intentions are casting, are determined to help, come what may. The results are not necessarily destructive, but they are deceptive in not being the effective psychotherapy that they seem to be. Many eager helpers are seduced into practising under the umbrella of psychotherapy without ever realising what it means that they encounter the psyche in that undertaking. Even if the content of the work seems clear, they do not grasp the nature of their material. With a conscience-free ignorance, psychotherapy is equated with helping, and this attractive prospect is taken for granted without further consideration of what help means. It is the present playground for hysteric deception.

The discovery that talking in the practice of psychotherapy may be dramatically effective in seeming to solve conflicts and remove unwelcome tensions is an exhilarating experience. Like a religious conversion, it is archetypally charged and open to the hazard of identifying with the process; open, that is, to a compulsion to 'go and do likewise' before realising the danger that it means, 'I, too, must be a saviour for those in distress'. History confirms that, when hysteria catches the attention, there is a tendency to see hysteria everywhere. In other words, when the saviour/helper is in the service of hysteria, it begins to look as if 'everyone needs help and must be helped'. Those who have been 'converted' flock towards psychotherapeutics of whatever calling and impose themselves on a correspondingly gullible public. But the question, 'who is helping whom', though obvious in most situations of need, is not self-evident in psychotherapy. Little note is taken of the suitability to their calling,

117

with the result that a large part of the psychotherapeutic scene is more in the nature of therapy as fulfilment for the therapist than for the unsuspecting members of the public, who are always ready to receive help for almost everything except what they need. This phenomenon is not in itself hysteria, but it is part of an unrecognised hysteric scene. Its presence in psychotherapy is as little appreciated as the psyche itself.

The blind rush into therapeutics is not so much a problem of mistakes as of misunderstandings. It thrives on the compulsion to interfere and *do* things with an attitude directed towards giving help and curing. Though disguised as a virtue, this help may become a vice because it overlooks and shows little respect for the reality of self-regulation and healing in the psyche. Help of that nature knows what is best for the patients; but in an alarmingly high proportion of cases that means doing what the helpers know to be best. The helpers do not know. They could only know 'what is best' if they were the patients, and they are not. The compulsion to do something leaves no time or place to consider the subtle distinction between helping the patient and being helpful to the patient. One attitude belongs to an effective and important form of nursing while the other attitude is the essential requirement, not only of psychotherapy, but of all therapeutics.

Here, then, is yet another borderline dimmed by hysteria. In this instance it means that a failure to recognise the presence, let alone the reality, of the psyche decides whether therapy is or is not under the auspices of healing.

With regard to the recipients of help running into hysteric infection, there is no shortage of examples. Amongst them is one feature of contemporary culture that deserves a mark of special attention because of the peculiar way it exhibits the unmistakable characteristics of hysteria. It is the theme of sexual child abuse, a ready-made home for hysteria's most natural expression. This has become an urgent problem of the moment, attracting widespread concern from those authorities it involves as well as the public in general. It detracts in no way from its real importance that there is a corresponding urgency to become aware of the suspicious features it demonstrates. Rarely has a pattern of behaviour given rise to more explosive passion, more moral indignation and more obstinate opinions of 'rightness' than this misdemeanour. 'Cases' are delivered up to the departments of help with a speed more appropriate to the intensive care unit.

Child abuse looms large as one of the inevitable complications in a society suddenly turned sexually permissive. It is joined readily by other primitive traits quick to join the new-found permissiveness. Violence goes hand in hand with sex and self-indulgence of all kinds flourishes where there is little respect for instinct. The problems are real and of undisputed importance, but they are not the immediate concern of this essay; the topic is not the way of abuse itself but the way hysteria catches and exaggerates it to present the picture of yet another phenomenon of mass hysteria.

There are many different forms of sexual child abuse claiming either sex as the victims. The pattern that has been most successful in catching the fascination of the public is at present that of maidens abused by men. Fathers carry a large share of the disapproval and the crimes they and others are accused of bear the signs of a sort of rape. The coincidence of this pattern is striking; the sex, the maiden and the 'rape that is not quite a rape' are a certain draw for hysteria. The scene is tailored to an extravagant suggestibility and hysteric exaggeration. For those who catch a hint of the mass infection, it should not be difficult to grasp that the 'rape' – indeed the whole picture – is not exactly what it seems to be. The facts sound convincing, but it is not always so obvious where, when or how this rape took place.

Often the 'inquisitorial' manner of investigation is open to suspicion. In the context of hysteria it points to yet another witch hunt. Amongst the non-medical public, very few people are aware of the association with hysteria, yet even the daily press has commented on the likeness to a witch hunt in those very words. There are some features noticeable in the handling of child abuse which bear an unmistakable resemblance to that of the most iniquitous period in the history of hysteria. History has a way of repeating itself. The difficulty is that the theme of child abuse, like that of many other

119

behaviour patterns, may involve crime as well as psychopathology and its nature is such that the two are more readily confused with each other than in other behavioural situations. To be alert to the deception is just as important for the guardian of the law as for the psychotherapist.

Psychotherapists miss the needs of their patients if they take only as literal the tales of abuse from a distant childhood, for there is an hypnotic subtlety in the way that theme draws the attention towards the possible crime of a parent and loses sight proportionately of the valuable information it offers about the attitude, past and present, of the patient. Similarly those in the social services responsible for abused children may fall for a miscarriage of justice if righteous indignation assumes the literal truth of all they hear. There are traps for the unwary at every encounter with this best known of hysteria's deceptions. Recognition of hysteria does not put an end to sexual child abuse, does not even ameliorate any crime; but it does, or can, reveal the blinding strength of hysteric suggestion and restore the problem to realistic proportions, freeing it from the evils of witch hunting.

Hysteria has walked unannounced into the halls of healing through the front door. It catches the attention with a strong enthusiasm and casts its theatrical glitter on the scene, but confuses the borders of all it touches. Time will tell whether the relatively new and daily expanding field of psychotherapy will undergo the differentiation it needs into greater clarity and authority if, or when, hysteria withdraws from that scene.

The autonomous effect of the hysteric image, however elusive or deceptive it may have proved to be, has played a prominent part in the evolution of medical science and its practice. Is it too much to suppose that, since the singular characteristics attributed to hysteria can move the fate of medicine in this manner, they may, too, move the fate of individuals towards their destined goals? If that is true, then Janet's appeal not to give up the word 'hysteria' needs extending. It must include an appropriate recognition of hysteria's existence as an unlikely reality always to be reckoned with and respected for not being what it seems. It is a sobering thought to remember how impoverished the imagination would be if things were always as they seemed to be.

BIBLIOGRAPHY

If the importance of this subject were in need of confirmation, the sheer quantity of literature produced through the centuries would alone be sufficient without the supporting evidence of a sharp rise in the output since the role of hysteria in medicine began its decline in recent decades. This bibliography gives a collection of books, dissertations and articles from authors in Europe and America ranging from the writings of past centuries to some of the most recent publications. It lends weight to the importance of the history for this subject as an indispensable study for any who may wish to understand the significance of hysteria today.

Abbot, E. Carl (1993) 'The wicked womb', *Canadian Medical Association Journal* 148 (3): 381–2.

Abrahams, K. (1927) 'Hysterical dream states', *Selected Papers*, London: Institute of Psychoanalysis/Hogarth Press.

Amsell, Gaston (1907) 'Conception de l'hystérie: Etude historique et clinique', Paris: Doin.

Babinski, J. and Froment, J. (1918) *Hysteria or Pithiasm and Reflex Nervous Disorders in the Neurology of War*, London: University of London Press.

Bart, Pauline B. and Scully, Diane H. (1979) 'The politics of hysteria: the case of the wandering womb', in E. S. Gomby and V. Franks (eds) *Gender and Disordered Behaviour: Sex Differences in Psychopathology*, New York: Brunner/Mazel.

de Beauvoir, Simone (1964) *The Second Sex*, trans. H. M. Parshley, London: Bantam Books.

Bercherie, Paul (1983) 'Le concept de la folie hystérique avant Charcot', *Revue internationale d'histoire de psychiatrie* 1 (1): 47–58.

Bitter, Wilhelm (1954) 'Die Hysterieforschung der "Französischen

Schule" und Neurosenlehre von Breuer und Freud', in *Psychotherapie und Seelsorge: Eine Einführung in die Tiefenpsychologie, gesammelte Vorträge*, Stuttgart: Gemeinschaft 'Arzt und Seelsorger'.

Blackmore, Sir Richard (1725) *A Treatise on the Spleen and Vapours: or, Hypochondriacal and Hysterical Affections*, London: Pemberton.

Bleuler, E. (1923) *Lehrbuch der Psychatrie*, Berlin: Verlag von Julius Springer: 412–23.

Boss, J. M. N. (1979) 'The seventeenth century transformation of the hysteric affection and Sydenham's Baconic medicine', *Journal of Psychological Medicine* 9.

Brain, Lord Russell (1963)'The Concept of Hysteria in the Times of William Harvey', *Proceedings of the Royal Society of Medicine* LVI.

Bresler, Johann (1896–7) 'Kulturhistorischer Beitrag zur Hystérie', *Allgemeine Zeitschrift für Psychiatrie* 53: 333–76.

Breuer, Joseph and Freud, Sigmund (1957) 'Studies on Hysteria', *Complete Psychological Works of Sigmund Freud*, vol. 2, London: Hogarth Press.

Briguet, P. (1859) *Traite clinique et thérapeutique de l'hystérie*, Paris: J. B. Baillière.

Brill, A. A. (1912) 'Hysterical dreaming states', *New York Medical Journal* XCV.

Bruttin, Jean-Marie (1969) *Différentes théories sur l'hystérie dans la première moitié du X1Xe siècle*, Zürich: Juris Druck.

Carroy-Thirard, Jacqueline (1979) 'Figure des femmes hystériques dans la psychiatrie française du 19e siècle', *Psychoanalyse à université* 4 (14): 313–24.

Cesbron, Henri (1909) *Histoire critique de l'hystérie*, Paris: Asselin et Houzeau.

Catonné, Jean-Philippe (1992) 'Femmes et hystérie au X1Xe siècle'. *Synapse* 88: 33–43.

Charcot, Jean-Martin (1991[1889]) *Clinical Lectures on Diseases of the Nervous System*, trans. T. Savill, ed. Ruth Harris, London and New York: Tavistock/Routledge.

—— (1969) *A propos de six cas d'hystérie chez l'homme*, Paris: Théraplix.

Chertok, Léon (1983) 'A l'occasion d'un centenaire Charcot: l'hystérie et l'hypnose', *Perspectives psychiatriques* 21 (2): 81–9.

Critchley, E. M. R. and Cantor, H. E. (1984) 'Charcot's hysteria renaissant', *British Medical Journal* 289 (6460): 1785–8.

Cumston, Charles G. (n. d.) *A Note on Dr. Charles Lepois' Writings on Hysteria*, London: Wellcome Institute for the History of Medicine, Reprints Collection.

Didi-Huberman, Georges (1982) *Invention de l'hystérie: Charcot et l'Iconographie photographique de la Salpetrière*, Paris: Macula.

124

Ellenberger, H. F. (1951) 'A propos du Malleus Maleficarum', *Schweizerische Zeitschrift für Psychologie* 10: 136–48.

—— (1970) *Discovery of the Unconscious*, London: Allen Lane.

Evans, Martha Noel (1991) *Fits and Starts: A Genealogy of Hysteria in Modern France*, Ithaca, NY: Cornell University Press.

Ey, Henri (1964) 'Introduction à l'étude actuelle d'hystérie', *Revue du practicien* 14 (11): 1417–31.

Ferenczi, S. (1926) 'The phenomena of hysterical materialization'; 'An attempted explanation of some hysterical stigmata'; The psychoanalysis of a case of hysterical hypochondria'; 'Materialization in Globus Hystericau', *Further Contributions to the Theorie and Technique of Psychoanalysis*, London: Institute of Psychoanalysis/Hogarth Press.

Fischer-Homberger, Esther (1969) 'Hysterie und Misogynie: Ein Aspekt der Hysteriegeschichte', *Gesnerus* 26 (1/2): 117–27.

Foucault, M. (1965) *Madness and Civilization*, New York: Pantheon.

Freud, S. (1924a) 'The aetiology of hysteria', *Collected Papers I*, London: Institute of Psychoanalysis/Hogarth Press.

—— (1924b) 'General remarks on hysterical attacks', *Collected Papers II*.

—— (1962) *A General Introduction to Psychoanalysis*, New York: Washington Square Press.

Gilman, S. L., King, H., Porter, R., Rousseau, G. and Showalter, E. (1993) *Hysteria Beyond Freud*, Berkeley: University of California Press.

Gobbi, Jean-Pierre (1985) 'Le Retour à Briquet: enquête sur la disparition de la notion d'hystérie', *Dianostic and Statistical Manual of Mental Disorders*, edn 3, Ph.D. dissertation, University of Paris VI.

Goblot, Jean-Jacques (1979) 'Extase, hystérie, possession: les théories d'Alexandre Bertrand', *Romantisme* 24: 53–9.

Gordon, E. *et al.* (1984) 'The development of hysteria as a psychiatric concept', *Comprehensive Psychiatry* 25 (5): 532–7.

Haberberg, Georges (1979) 'De Charcot à Babinski. Etude du rôle de l'hystérie dans la naissance de la neurologie moderne', Ph.D. dissertation, University of Paris, Créteil.

Havens, Leston L. (1966) 'Charcot and hysteria', *Journal of Nervous and Mental Diseases* 141 (5): 505–16.

Hawkins, Ernest L. (1978) 'The raging womb: an archetypal study of hysteria and the early psychoanalytic movement', Ph.D. dissertation, University of Dallas.

Hellpack, W. (1904) *Grundlinien einer Psychologie der Hysterie*, Leipzig: Wilhelm Engelmann.

125

Hillman, J. H. (1972) *The Myth of Analysis*, Evanston, Ill.: Northwestern University Press: 251–85.

Imbert, P. (1931) 'Le problème de l'hystérie dans le passé'. Ph.D. dissertation, University of Nancy.

Janet, P. (1893) 'Quelques définitions recentes de hystérie', *Archives de Neurologie* 25 (76 & 77).

—— (1901) *The Mental States of Hystericals: A Study of Mental Stigmata and Mental Accidents*, trans. R. C. Carson, New York: Putnam & Sons.

Jaspers, K. (1972) *General Psychopathology*, Manchester: Manchester University Press.

Johnson, W. (1849) *An Essay on Disease of Young Women*, London: Simkin Marshall: 5.

Jones, E. (1913) 'The Relation between Anxiety Neurosis and Anxiety Hysteria', *Papers on Psychoanalysys*, New York: Wood & Co.

Jorden, E. (1971[1603]) *A Brief Discourse of a Disease called the Suffocation of the Mother*, New York: De Capo Press [London: John Windet].

Jung, C. G. (1902) 'On the Psychology of so-called Occult Phenomena', trans. R. C. F. Hull, in *Collected Works*, vol. 1, London: Routledge & Kegan Paul.

—— (1906) 'Freud's Theory of Hysteria: A Reply to Aschaffenberg', *Collected Works*.

—— (1908) 'The Freudian Theory of Hysteria', *Collected Works*.

King, Helen, (1985) 'From Parthenos to Gynē: the dynamics of category', Ph.D. dissertation, University College, London.

—— (1993) 'Once upon a text: hysteria from Hippocrates', in S. L. Gilman *et al.*, *Hysteria beyond Freud*, Berkeley, University of California Press.

Kloë, Elisabeth (1979) 'Hysterie im Kindesalter: Zur Entwicklung des kindlichen Hysteriebegriffes', in *Freiburger Forschungen zur Medizinegeschichte*, vol. 9, Freiburg: Hans Ferdinand Schultz.

Knoff, William F. (1971) 'Four thousand years of hysteria', *Comprehensive Psychiatry* 12 (2): 156–64.

Kraemer, R. (1932) *Der Wandel in den wissenschaftlichen Anschaungen über Hysterie unter besonderer Berücksichtigung der letzten Jahrzehnte*, Würzburg.

Krohn, Alan (1978) *Hysteria: The Elusive Neurosis*, Monograph 45/46 of *Psychological Issue* 12 (1/2), New York: International Universities Press.

Leibbrand, Annemarie and Leibbrand, Werner (1975) 'Die Kopernikanische Wendung des Hysteriebegriffes bei Paracelsus', in Sepp

Domandl (ed.) *Paracelsus: Werk und Wirkung*, Salzburger Beiträger zur Paracelsusforschung, vol. 13, Vienna: WGO.

Levin, Kenneth (1971) 'S. Weir Mitchell: investigations and insights into neurasthenia and hysteria', *Transactions and Studies of the College of Physicians of Philadelphia* 38 (3): 168–73.

Lewis, Sir Aubrey (1975) 'The survival of hysteria', *Psychological Medicine* 5 (1): 9–12.

Libbrecht, Katrien (1994) *Hysterical Psychosis: An Historical Survey*, New Brunswick, NJ: Transaction Books 1994.

McGrath, William J. (1986) *Freud's Discovery of Psychoanalysis: The Politics of Hysteria*, Ithaca, NY: Cornell University Press.

Mai, François M. and Merskey, Harold (1978) 'Briquet's concept of hysteria: an historical perspective', *Canadian Journal of Psychiatry* 19 (1): 57–63.

Meares, Russell *et al.* (1983) 'Whose hysteria: Briquet's, Janet's or Freud's?', *Australian and New Zealand Journal of Psychiatry* 19 (3): 265–73.

Mehren, G. (1988) 'Hysterie und Ekstase', Diploma Thesis, C. G. Jung Institut, Zürich.

Merskey, H. (1979) *The Analysis of Hysteria*. London: Baillière Tindall.

—— (1986) 'The Importance of Hysteria', *British Journal of Psychiatry* 149: 23–8.

—— (1993) 'Hysteria, or Suffocation of the Mother', *Canadian Medical Association Journal* 148 (3): 399–455.

Micale, Mark S (1989) 'Hysteria and its historiography – A review of past and present writings', 2 parts, *History of Science* 27 (77): 223–61; 27 (78): 317–51.

—— (1990a) 'Charcot and the idea of hysteria in the male: Gender, mental science and medical diagnosis in late nineteenth-century France', *Medical History* 34 (4): 363–411.

—— (1990b) 'Hysteria and its hysteriography: The feature perspective', *History of Psychiatry* 1 (1): 33–124.

—— (1993) 'On the disappearance of hysteria: A study in the Clinical deconstruction of a diagnosis', *Isis* 84: 496–526.

Micklem, N. (1974) *On Hysteria: The Mythical Syndrome*, New York: Spring Publications.

Moebius, P. J. (1888) 'Über den Begriff der Hysterie', *Zentralblatt für Nervenheilkunde* 2.

Mullen, John (1984) 'Hypochondria and hysteria: sensibility and the physicians', *The 18th Century: Theory and Interpretation* 25 (2) 141–74.

Oppenheim, H. (1890) 'Tatsächliches und Hypothetisches über das Wesen der Hysterie', *Berliner Klinische Wochenschrift* 27.

Palis, J., Rossopoulos, E. and Triarhou, L. (1985) 'The Hippocratic concept of hysteria: a translation of the oringinal texts', *Integrative Psychiatry* 3 (3): 226–8.

Plato (1892) 'Timaeus', *Dialogues of Plato*, vol. 3, trans. B. Jowett, Oxford: Clarendon Press.

Purcell, John. (1707) *A Treatise of Vapours, or Hysterick Fits*, London: E. Place.

Roy, Alec (1982) (ed.) *Hysteria*, Chichester: John Wiley & Sons.

Savill, T. D. (1909) *Lectures on Hysteria and allied Vasomotor Conditions*, New York: William Wood & Co.

Schapira, L. L. (1988) *The Cassandra Complex. A Modern Perspective on Hysteria*, Toronto: Inner City Books.

Schaps, Regina. (1982) *Hysterie und Weiblichkeit: Wissenschaftsmythen über die Frau*, Frankfurt: Campus.

Schneck, J. (1957) 'Thomas Sydenham and psychological medicine', *American Journal of Psychiatry* 13: 1034.

Schneider, Manfried (1985) 'Hysterie als Gesamtkunstwerk', in Alfred Pfabigon (ed.) *Ornament und Askese im Zeitgeist des Wien Jahrhundertwende*, Vienna: Brandstätter.

Schrenk, Martin (1974) 'Über Hysterie und Hysterie-Forscher', *Praxis der Psychotherapie* 19 (6): 250–62.

Sentuc, Anne (1985) 'Mysticisme hystérique ou hystérie mystique?' *Historama* 22: 83–5.

Shorter, Edward (1984) 'Les désordres psychosomatiques: Sont-ils "hystériques"? Notes pour une récherche historique', *Cahiers internationaux de sociologie* 76: 201–24.

Showalter, Elaine (1987) *The Female Malady*, London: Virago.

Simon, Bennett (1979) 'Hysteria – the Greek disease', *Psychoanalytic Study of Society* 8: 175–215.

Slavney, Phillip R. (1990) *Perspectives on 'Hysteria'*, Baltimore Md: The Johns Hopkins University Press.

Small, S. Mouchly (1969) 'Concept of hysteria: history and re-evaluation', *New York State Journal of Medicine* 69: 1866–72.

Strong, Beret E. (1989) 'Foucault, Freud, and French feminism: theorizing hysteria as theorizing the feminine', *Literature and Psychology* 35 (4): 10–17.

Sydenham, Thomas (1848) *The Works of Thomas Sydenham MD*, trans. from Latin edition of Dr Greenhill with a 'Life of the Author' by R. G. Letten, London.

Syndor, Denise Newman (1991) 'Hysteria: a historical perspective'. Ph.D. dissertation, Miami Institute of Psychology.

Trillat, Etienne (1984) 'Sur la naissance de l'hystérie de Charcot', *Perspectives psychiatriques* 96 (2): 137–41.

—— (1986) *Histoire de l'hystérie*, Paris: Seghers.

Veith, Ilza (1965) *Hysteria: The History of a Disease*, Chicago: University of Chicago Press.

Walshe, Sir Francis (1963) *Diseases of the Nervous System*, 10th edn, Livingston: 361.

Wesley, George Randolf (1979) *A History of Hysteria*, Washington, DC: University Press of America.

Wettley, Annemarie (1969) 'Hysterie, ärztliche Einbildung oder Wirklichkeit', *Müncher Medizinische Wochenschrift* 101: 193–6.

Whyatt, Robert (1767) *Observations on the Nature, Causes and Cure of those Disorders which have been commonly called Nervous, Hypochondriac or Hysteric*, 3rd edn, Edinburgh: J. Balfour: 85.

Williams, M. (1956) 'A study of hysteria in women', *Journal of Analytic Psychology* 12.

INDEX